"If Rachel Hollis tells you to wash your face, turn on that water! She is the mentor every woman needs, from new mommas to seasoned business women."

—**ANNA TODD,** *New York Times* and #1 internationally
bestselling author of the After series

"Rachel's voice is the winning combination of an inspiring life coach and your very best (and funniest) friend. Shockingly honest and hilariously down to earth, *Girl, Wash Your Face* is a gift to women who want to flourish and live a courageously authentic life."

—**MEGAN TAMTE,** founder and co-CEO of Evereve

"There aren't enough women in leadership telling other women to GO FOR IT. We typically get the caregiver; we rarely get the boot camp instructor. Rachel lovingly but firmly tells us it is time to stop letting the tail wag the dog and get on with living our wild and precious lives. *Girl, Wash Your Face* is a dose of high-octane straight talk that will spit you out on the other end, chasing down dreams you hung up long ago. Love this girl."

—**JEN HATMAKER,** *New York Times* bestselling
author of *For the Love* and *Of Mess and Moxie* and
happy online hostess to millions every week

"In Rachel Hollis's first nonfiction book, you will find she is less cheerleader and more life coach. This means readers won't just walk away inspired; they will walk away with the right tools in hand to actually do their dreams. Dream *doing* is what Rachel is all about. You will be, too, when you read her newest book."

—**JESSICA HONEGGER,** founder and
co-CEO of the Noonday Collection

"Rachel has one of those rare abilities to make you laugh out loud and also completely rethink your entire life all in one paragraph. Her words and this book are a gift and we know they'll encourage and challenge you deeply."

—JEFFERSON AND ALYSSA BETHKE, *New York Times* bestselling authors of *Jesus>Religion* and *Love That Lasts*

Girl, wash your face

Girl, wash your face

Stop Believing the Lies About Who You Are So You Can Become Who You Were Meant to Be

RACHEL HOLLIS

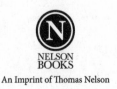

NELSON
BOOKS

An Imprint of Thomas Nelson

Published in Nashville, Tennessee, by Nelson Books, an imprint of Thomas Nelson. Nelson Books and Thomas Nelson are registered trademarks of HarperCollins Christian Publishing, Inc.

Thomas Nelson titles may be purchased in bulk for educational, business, fundraising, or sales promotional use. For information, please e-mail SpecialMarkets@ ThomasNelson.com.

Any Internet addresses, phone numbers, or company or product information printed in this book are offered as a resource and are not intended in any way to be or to imply an endorsement by Thomas Nelson, nor does Thomas Nelson vouch for the existence, content, or services of these sites, phone numbers, companies, or products beyond the life of this book.

Unless otherwise noted, Scripture quotations are taken from the Holy Bible, New International Version®, NIV®. Copyright © 1973, 1978, 1984, 2011 by Biblica, Inc.™ Used by permission of Zondervan. All rights reserved worldwide. www.zondervan.com. The "NIV"and "New International Version" are trademarks registered in the United States Patent and Trademark Office by Biblica, Inc.™

Scripture quotations marked WEB are taken from the World English Bible. Public domain.

ISBN 978-1-4002-0166-2 (eBook)

Library of Congress Cataloging-in-Publication Data

ISBN 978-1-4002-0165-5
Library of Congress Control Number: 2017949726

Printed in the United States of America

18 19 20 21 22 LSC 40

For Jen, who has shaken my worldview off its axis three times: once with *Interrupted*, once with a trip to Ethiopia, and lastly by teaching us all that a *real* leader speaks the truth, even to her own detriment.

CONTENTS

CONTENTS

INTRODUCTION

Hey Girl, Hey!

This is the big opening letter to my book, the part where I tell you all the things I'm hoping for as you read it. This is the moment where I outline my intentions and—if you're already game to read on—this is where I fire you up more about what to anticipate. This is also the important letter for someone standing in the bookstore right now trying to decide if she should buy this book or, like, *The Life-Changing Magic of Tidying Up*—and the words she's reading now will decide for her. I mean, that feels like a lot of pressure for one little letter, but here we go.

This book is about a bunch of hurtful lies and one important truth.

The truth? You, and only you, are ultimately responsible for who you become and how happy you are. That's the takeaway.

Don't get me wrong. I'm going to tell a hundred stories that are funny or weird or embarrassing or sad or crazy, but each of them is reaching for this same pithy, Pinterest-worthy truth: your life is up to *you*.

But that truth will never be believable if you don't first understand the lies that get in the way of it. Understanding that you choose your own happiness, that you have control of your own life, is so important. It's one of those things we grasp with both hands and put up on the bulletin board as a reminder . . . but it's not the only thing you need to understand.

You also need to identify—and systematically destroy—every lie you've told yourself your whole life.

Why?

Because it's impossible to go somewhere new, to *become* something new, without first acknowledging where you are. The self-awareness that comes from truly digging into what you've come to believe about who you are is invaluable.

Have you ever believed that you aren't good enough? That you're not thin enough? That you're unlovable? That you're a bad mom? Have you ever believed that you deserve to be treated badly? That you'll never amount to anything?

All lies.

All lies perpetuated by society, the media, our family of origin, or frankly—and this is my Pentecostal showing—by the Devil himself. These lies are dangerous and devastating to our sense of worth and our ability to function. The most sinister thing about them is that we rarely hear them at all. We rarely hear the lies we've created about ourselves because they've been playing so loudly in our ears for so long that they've become white noise. The hateful narrative bombards us every day, yet we don't even realize it's there. Recognizing the lies we've come to accept about ourselves is the key to growing into a better version of ourselves. If we can identify the core of our struggles while simultaneously understanding that we are truly in control of conquering them, then we can utterly change our trajectory.

That's why I do what I do. That's why I run a website and talk about how to make a centerpiece, or parent with kindness, or strengthen a marriage. It's why I researched thirty different ways to clean out your front-load washer before I taught my tribe how to do it. It's why I know the perfect ratio of balsamic and citrus to make your pot roast taste amazing. Sure, I cover a whole host of topics using my online platform, but ultimately they boil down to one thing: these are the elements of my life, and I want to do them well. The posts demonstrate how I am growing and learning, and I want them to grow and encourage other women too. I suppose if I'd been into homeschooling or knitting or photography or macramé, I would have used those things to try and better myself and boost up my friends. But I'm not into those things. I'm into lifestyle stuff, so I focus on creating content that falls under the banner of lifestyle media.

Early on in this career, though, I realized that a lot of women look at lifestyle imagery as what they *should* aspire to be. Many of those images are impossible—another lie foisted upon us—so I set out to be honest from the beginning. I vowed to be authentic and sincere, and for every gloriously styled cupcake picture we produced, I shared a photo of myself with facial paralysis. If I went somewhere fancy like the Oscars, I balanced that with a post about my struggle with weight loss and pictures of me forty pounds heavier. I've talked about it all: struggles in my marriage, postpartum depression, and feeling jealous, scared, angry, ugly, unworthy, unloved. I have tried to be totally real about who I am and where I'm coming from. Seriously, the most famous thing I've ever done was to post a picture of the stretch marks on my saggy tummy on the internet. And yet . . .

And yet I still get the notes. Women from all over the world still email and ask me how I manage to keep it all together while they struggle. I can *feel* the pain in those emails. I can hear the shame in the words they use to describe their own hardships, and it makes my heart hurt.

So I write them back. I tell every single one how beautiful and strong she is. I call them *warrior, courageous, fighter.* I tell them not to give up. It's what feels appropriate to say to a total stranger. But it's not all I want to say. It's not what I would say if it were my sister who was hurting, or my best friend. It's not what I wish I could say to my younger self. Because to those closest to me, I am supportive and encouraging . . . but I absolutely refuse to watch you wallow.

The truth is that *you are* strong and courageous and a fighter . . . but if I'm telling you that, it's because I want you to see those characteristics in yourself. I want to grab you by the shoulders and shake you until your teeth rattle. I want to get in your face until you have the courage to look me in the eyes and see the answer for yourself. I want to shout at the top of my lungs until you know this one great truth: you are in control of your own life. You get one and only one chance to live, and life is passing you by. Stop beating yourself up, and dang it, stop letting others do it too. Stop accepting less than you deserve. Stop buying things you can't afford to impress people you don't even really like. Stop eating your feelings instead of working through them. Stop buying your kids' love with food, or toys, or friendship because it's easier than parenting. Stop abusing your body and your mind. Stop! Just get off the never-ending track. Your life is supposed to be a journey from one unique place to another; it's not supposed to be a merry-go-round that brings you back to the same spot over and over again.

Your life doesn't have to look like mine. Heck, your life doesn't have to look like anyone else's at all, but it should at least be a creation of your own making.

Is it going to be hard? Absolutely! But taking the easy way out is how you end up on the sofa, fifty pounds overweight, while life passes you by.

Will change happen overnight? No way! This is a lifelong process. You'll try out some different tools and techniques, and while some of them will feel okay, maybe one will feel like the answer and then thirty-seven different others will feel like garbage. Then you'll wake up tomorrow and do it again. And again. And again.

And you'll fail.

You'll fall off the wagon. You'll eat half of a birthday cake when no one is watching or scream at your husband or drink too much wine all month long. You'll fall into ruts because this is life and that's just how it goes. But once you understand that *you* are the one who is truly in control, you'll get up and try again. And you'll keep going until being in control feels more natural than being out of control. It'll become a way of life, and you'll become the person you are meant to be.

It's worth asking, right here, right up front, where faith plays a role in all of this. As a Christian I grew up learning that God was in control, that God had a plan for my life, and I believe in the marrow of my bones that this is true. I believe God loves each of us unconditionally, but I don't think that means we get to squander the gifts and talents he's given us simply because we're good enough already. A caterpillar is awesome, but if the caterpillar stopped there—if she just decided that *good* is *good enough*—we would all miss out on the beautiful creature she would become.

You are more than you have become.

That's what I want to tell the women who write to me asking for advice. It might be tough to hear, but that knowledge is followed by this sweet truth: you are more than you have become, and you are utterly in control over what you do with that knowledge.

Which led me to an idea.

What if I wrote a whole book about all the ways I have struggled and then explained the steps that helped me get past those times? What if I talked about all of my failures and embarrassing moments? What if you knew that my biggest shame is that I sometimes get so angry I scream at my children? Not holler, not yell, not scold them strongly, but scream so loudly it nauseates me to think of it later. What if you hear that I likely have at least three cavities in my mouth right now because I am petrified of the dentist? What if I talked about my cellulite, or the weird third boob thing that sits in between my arm and my regular boob when I wear a tank top? Did I mention back fat? Or the hair that grows out of the mole on my face? Or my insecurities? What if I started a book by telling you that I peed my pants as an adult, as a fully grown human, and it wasn't the first time, nor will it be the last? And what if I told you that even in spite of my confessions—be they funny, embarrassing, painful, or gross—I am at peace with myself? That I love who I am even when I do things I'm not proud of? And that it's possible because I know I am ultimately in control of making change? I am in control over the person I will become. By the grace of God, I will wake up tomorrow and have another chance to do this life better. By the grace of God, I've had thirty-five years of *trying* so hard in some areas of my life (like the creation of cheese-based casseroles) that I am crushing it. And in other areas (like controlling my anxiety)

I am constantly working on different angles to attack the same problem.

It's a lifelong journey, but I rest in the knowledge that every day I'm learning and growing, which lets me feel at peace with myself.

The things I've struggled with? The lies I've believed about myself for so long?

The list is a mile long. So long, in fact, that I decided to dedicate a chapter to each one. Every single section of this book begins with a lie that I believed, and what follows are the stories of how that particular lie held me back, hurt me, and in some cases, caused me to hurt others. But by admitting to these lies, I have taken their power away. I'll share with you how I made changes in my life to overcome the struggles—some for good, and some as an ever-evolving dance between myself and lifelong insecurities.

What are my insecurities? Well, here are some of the biggest and the baddest in no particular order. I hope they'll encourage you. I hope you'll find the ideas helpful. More than anything, I hope you'll rest in the knowledge that you can become whomever and whatever you want to be, my sweet friend. And on the days that seem the hardest, you'll remember that—by an inch or a mile—forward momentum is the only requirement.

love,
Rach

CHAPTER 1

The lie:

SOMETHING ELSE WILL MAKE ME HAPPY

I peed my pants last week.

Not *full-on* peed my pants, like that one time at summer camp when I was ten years old. We were playing capture the flag, and I couldn't hold it a second longer. I didn't want to admit that I'd just wet my pants, so I doused myself with a bottle of water. Imagine, if you will, that once all of my clothes were wet, no one—most especially Christian Clark, my camp crush—was the wiser. I was resourceful even then.

Did others find it odd that I was suddenly soaking wet?

Probably.

But I'd rather be an oddball than a pants-wetter any day of the week.

As for last week, this wasn't *that* level of peeing my pants. This was just your regular I've-pushed-three-babies-out-of-my-body dribbling.

Giving birth to a baby is like a space shuttle launch. Everything gets destroyed on the way out, which means that sometimes, you guys, I pee my pants. If this knowledge hurts your tender sensibilities, then I'm going to assume you haven't had bladder-control problems—and I offer you my congratulations. However, if my experience makes sense to you, then you probably have this problem too—which means you just laughed a little, having experienced a similar predicament.

I was jumping with my boys out back, and somebody hollered for me to show off a midair toe touch. This is my only known skill on a trampoline, and if I'm going to work up the gumption to hoist myself onto that spring-loaded death trap, you'd better believe I'm going to give it my all. One second I was soaring through the air like one of the extra-tiny gals they launch into basket tosses during a cheerleading competition, and the next moment my pants were wet. Nobody noticed—unless you count my pride—but it happened just the same. I had to keep jumping so that the continuous wind rush would dry out my shorts. I'm resourceful, remember? The timing was perfection, too, because not thirty minutes later, a previously programmed Facebook post went up showing me trying on dresses for the Oscars.

Before you get the wrong impression, I am not fancy enough to go to the Academy Awards. I am, however, married to someone ultra hunky. He's not really fancy either, but his job certainly is. That means that sometimes I get to wear dresses like a princess and drink free wine in well-lit ballrooms. In these instances, photos show up on Instagram or Facebook of us looking well coiffed and ultra glam, and the internet goes wild. This is prime real estate for people to write me notes about how glamorous my life is, how stylish and fashionable and perfect my world must be. And all I can think when I read those comments later is, *I've just peed myself, in public, surrounded by other human beings.* I've literally gone to the bathroom *in the air* while trying to force my hamstrings into unnatural gymnastic positions in order to impress my three-year-old.

Y'all, I'm about as unglamorous as you can get.

And I don't mean that in a celebrity, *stars-are-just-like-us* kind of way. This is not like that time Gwyneth went makeup-free and, with her perfect skin and her angel-blonde hair, tried to convince us she was just a regular gal even in her four-hundred-dollar T-shirt.

No, I mean this literally.

I am not glamorous. I am 1,000 percent one of the nerdiest people you're likely to meet. If I've somehow managed to convince you otherwise because I run a lifestyle website with pretty pictures, or because my hair looks extra shiny on Instagram sometimes, well, sister, let me set you straight. I am not a perfect wife, not a perfect mother, not a perfect friend or boss, and most definitely not a perfect Christian. Not. Even. Close. I'm not perfect at anything I do—well, except for making and eating dishes that are primarily cheese-based—but the other stuff, the *life* stuff? Oh girl, I'm struggling.

I feel like it's important to say that. Important enough to base an entire book around the idea, in fact, because I want to make sure you *hear it.*

I am so incredibly flawed in big ways and small ways and sideways and beside ways, and *I make a living telling other women how to better their lives.* Me—of the workout regimens and DIY skin-brightening scrub. Me—with the tips on cooking Thanksgiving dinner and the itemized list of how to parent your kids. Me—I am failing.

All. The. Time.

This is important because I want you to understand, my sweet, precious friend, that *we're all falling short*. Yet even though I fail over and over and over again, I don't let it deter me. I still wake up every day and try again to become a better version of myself. Some days I feel as if I'm getting closer to the best version of me. Other days I eat cream cheese for dinner. But the gift of life is that we get another chance tomorrow.

Somewhere along the way women got the wrong information. Or, I should say, we got *so much* of the wrong information that we washed our hands of the whole thing. We live in an all-or-nothing society that says I need to look, act, think, and speak perfectly or just throw in the towel and stop trying altogether.

That's what I worry about the most—that you've stopped trying. I get notes from readers and see thousands of comments on my social media feeds. Some of you feel so overwhelmed by your life that you've given up. You're a piece of jetsam being tugged along with the tide. It feels too hard to keep up with the game, so you've quit playing. Oh sure, you're still here. You still show up for work, you still make dinner and take care of your kids, but you're always playing catch-up. You always feel behind and overwhelmed.

Life is not supposed to overwhelm you at all times. Life isn't meant to be merely survived—it's meant to be *lived*.

Seasons or instances will inevitably feel out of your control, but the moments when you feel like you're drowning are supposed to be brief. They should not be the whole of your existence! The precious life you've been given is like a ship navigating its way across the ocean, and you're meant to be the captain of the vessel. Certainly there are times when storms toss you around or cover the deck with water or break the mast clean in half— but that's when you need to fight your way back, to throw all the water off the boat bucket by bucket. That's when you battle to get yourself back to the helm. This is *your* life. You are meant to be the hero of your own story.

This doesn't mean you become selfish. This doesn't mean you discard your faith or quit believing in something greater than yourself. What it means is taking responsibility for your own life and your own happiness. Said another way—a harsher, more-likely-to-get-me-punched-in-the-face way—if you're unhappy, *that's on you.*

When I say unhappy, I mean *unhappy.* I don't mean *depressed.* True depression has everything to do with your genetic makeup and the chemical balance in your body. As someone who's battled depression personally, I have the utmost compassion for anyone who's going through it. I also don't mean *sadness.* Sadness or grief brought on by circumstances outside of your control—like the soul-shredding loss of a loved one—is not something that can be walked through quickly or easily. Sadness and pain are things you have to sit with and get to know or you'll never be able to move on.

When I say unhappy, I mean discontented, unsettled, frus-trated, angry—any of a number of emotions that make us want to hide from our lives instead of embracing them with arms wide open like a Creed song. Because happy people—the ones who are enjoying their lives 90 percent of the time—do exist. You've seen them. In fact, you're reading a book written by one right now.

Ultimately, I think that's what people are commenting on in my photos. They're saying, "Your life looks so perfect," but what I think they mean is, "Your life seems happy. You look content. You're always optimistic and grateful. You're always laughing."

I want to explain why . . .

I didn't have an easy start. Actually, if I am being honest, the word I would use to describe much of my childhood is *traumatic*. Our house was chaotic—the highest highs and the lowest lows. There were big parties filled with family and friends, followed by screaming and fighting and crying. Fist-sized holes would find their way into the walls, and plates would shatter against the kitchen floor. My father handled stress with anger; my mother handled it by going to bed for weeks at a time. Like most children who grow up similarly, I didn't know there was any other way to be a family.

Then, when I was fourteen years old, my big brother, Ryan, committed suicide. The things I saw and went through that day will haunt me forever, but they also changed me in a fundamental way. I was the baby of four children and had spent my life up until that point largely ignorant of the world outside my own home. But when Ryan died, our already turbulent and troubled home shattered. If life was difficult before he died, it was untenable afterward.

I grew up in that single day. And amid the anguish and fear and confusion of his death, I recognized a great truth: if I wanted a better life than the one I'd been born into, it was up to me to create it.

The year he died I was a freshman in high school, and I immediately started taking as many classes as I could in order to graduate early. My junior year, I received my diploma and moved to Los Angeles, the closest major city to my small California hometown. To this country mouse, LA seemed like the kind of place where any dream could come true. I was seventeen years old, not even grown-up enough to get a phone line or sign the lease on my apartment without an adult signature, but all I could focus on was finally getting away. For years I'd lived within the chaos of my childhood home thinking, *Someday I'll get out of here, and then I'll be happy.*

How could I not be happy in LA? I soaked up every inch of it from the second my feet hit the ground. I absorbed the frenetic energy of Hollywood and adapted to the rhythm of the waves rolling to shore along PCH. A multidimensional skyline made me feel worldly. I appreciated the kind of views that only an outsider would see.

Most people don't notice the trees in Beverly Hills. They're much too busy coveting the mansions that sit below them, but the trees were one of the first things I saw. I gloried in beauty for the sake of beauty, since that sort of thing hadn't existed in the place where I'd grown up. The thing is, the trees all match in Beverly Hills. On any given street, around any given corner, and even amid the chaos of a bustling city, you will see row after row of perfect symmetry—a menagerie of Canary Island pines and camphor trees and date palms. They were laid out by the original landscape architect back at the beginning of the twentieth century. They hug the wide streets in meticulous rows, silent sentinels of one of the world's most affluent cities. After a lifetime of chaos, I delighted in the order.

Finally, I thought to myself, *I'm where I belong.*

Time passed and seasons changed, and my new city eventually taught me one of the most vital lessons I've ever learned. Moving or traveling or getting away? It's just geography. Moving doesn't change who you are. It only changes the view outside your window. You must *choose* to be happy, grateful, and fulfilled. If you make that choice every single day, regardless of where you are or what's happening, you will be happy.

I get to see my best friend, Amanda, a few times a year. Every time we hang out we talk until our throats are sore and laugh until our cheeks hurt. Amanda and I would have just as much fun hanging out in my living room as we would lying on a beach in Mexico. Now, granted, Mexico is prettier, the weather is nicer, and we'd have easier access to cocktails with little umbrellas in them . . . but we can have a great time whether we're in my back-yard or behind the Dumpster at the local Walmart because we're so excited to hang out with each other. When you're engaged and involved and choosing to enjoy your own life, it doesn't matter where you are, or frankly, what negative things get hurled at you. You'll still find happiness because it's not about *where* you are but *who* you are.

THINGS THAT HELPED ME . . .

1. *I stopped comparing myself.* I stopped comparing myself to other people, and I also stopped comparing myself to whomever I thought I was supposed to be. Comparison is the death of joy, and the only person you need to be better than is the one you were yesterday.

2. *I surrounded myself with positivity.* I cringe even writing that because it sounds like a poster you'd see taped to the wall of your eighth-grade gym class—but cheesy or not, it's gospel. You become who you surround yourself with. You become what you consume. If you find yourself in a slump or feel as though you're living in a negative space, take a good hard look at who and what you see every day.

3. *I figured out what makes me happy and I do those things.* This seems like the most obvious idea in the world,

but at the end of the day, very few people intentionally choose the things that bring them joy. No, I don't mean that you can build a life around massages and lavish dinners (or maybe you can, fancy pants!). I mean that you should spend more time doing things that feed your spirit: more long walks with your dog, less volunteering for that thing you feel obligated to do but actually hate. You are in charge of your own life, sister, and there's not one thing in it that you're not *allowing* to be there. Think about it.

CHAPTER 2

The Lie:

I'LL START TOMORROW

I can't count the number of diets I've tried. I can't tell you the number of times I've made plans to go to the gym and then blew them off. Number of half marathons I signed up for, paid the entry fee for, and then quietly pretended not to remember when it was time to actually train? Two. Number of times I've declared, "From here on out, I'm going to walk a mile every morning before work!" and then never made it past the third day?

Infinity.

I had this habit for years, as many women do. We talk about the things we'd like to do, be, try, and accomplish, but once we get to the moment of actually *doing it*, we fold faster than a card table after bunco night.

Maybe we've created this habit because we were brought up

observing this pattern. Magazines and TV shows spend a lot of time focusing on what to do when we fall off the wagon rather than teaching us how to stay on it in the first place. Life happens, and the plans we make fall through—but when it becomes such a regular occurrence that the promises we make hold very little actual power in our lives, we need to check ourselves.

A few months ago I was out to dinner with my closest girlfriends. It was an impromptu happy hour that turned into an impromptu dinner and ended up going later than any of us anticipated. I got home after the kids were in bed, and Dave was already deep into a game of Major League Ball or Hard Hitting League or whatever the name is of the baseball game he's played nightly for the last two years of our marriage (without making any real progress that I'm aware of). So I gave him a smooch and chatted with him about his day, then I went downstairs to the basement where our old treadmill is hidden and ran a few miles. I put the evidence of that workout on Snapchat, and later my girlfriend saw it and sent me a text. You worked out after dinner? What in the world?

I wrote back, Yes, because I planned on doing it and didn't want to cancel.

Couldn't you just postpone until tomorrow? She was genuinely perplexed.

No, because I made a promise to myself and I don't break those, not ever.

Ugh, she typed back. I'm the FIRST person I break a promise to.

She's not the only one. I used to do that all the time until I realized how hard I was fighting to keep my word to other people while quickly canceling on myself. *I'll work out tomorrow* became *I'm not working out anytime soon*—because honestly, if you really cared about that commitment, you'd do it when you said you would. What if you had a friend who constantly flaked on you? What if every other time you made plans she decided not to show up? What if she gave lame excuses like, "I really want to see you, but this TV show I'm watching is just so good"?

Or what if a friend from work was constantly starting something new? Every three Mondays she announced a new diet or goal and then two weeks later it just ended? What if you called her on it, like, "Hey, Pam, I thought you were doing Whole30"? Meanwhile Pam is sitting in the break room eating a meat lover's pizza and telling you that she *was* doing Whole30, and even though it made her feel great, two weeks into the program her son had a birthday party and she couldn't resist the cake and then figured there was no point. Now she's gained back the pounds she lost plus a few extra.

Y'all, would you respect her? This woman who starts and stops over and over again? Would you count on Pam or the friend who keeps blowing you off for stupid reasons? Would you trust them when they committed to something? Would you believe them when they committed to you?

No.

No way. And that level of distrust and apprehension applies to you too. Your subconscious knows that you, yourself, cannot be trusted after breaking so many plans and giving up on so many goals.

On the flip side, have you ever known someone who always kept their word? If they tell you they're coming, you can expect them ten minutes early. If they commit to a project, you can bet your butt they'll finish it. They tell you they've signed up for their first marathon, and you're already in awe because you know for a fact they'll finish. When this type of person commits to something, how seriously do you take their commitment?

I hope you see my point here.

If you constantly make and break promises to yourself, you're not making promises at all. You're talking. You're waxing poetic like Pam and her diet or your flaky friend who bails on you to watch *Game of Thrones*.

How many times have you bailed on yourself to watch TV? How many times have you given up before you've even started? How many times have you made real progress, only to face a setback and then give up completely? How many times have your family or friends or coworkers watched you quit? How many times have your children watched you give up on yourself over and over and over?

This is not okay.

Our society makes plenty of room for complacency or laziness; we're rarely surrounded by accountability. We're also rarely surrounded by sugar-free vanilla lattes, but when I really want one, I somehow find a way to get one.

I'm only sort of kidding.

When you really want something, you will find a way. When you don't really want something, you'll find an excuse. How does your subconscious know the difference between what you want and what you only pretend to want? It looks at a history of how you've tackled similar things in the past. Have you kept your word? When you set out to do something, did you see it through? When we're at a loss, we reach for the lowest bar—and the lowest bar is typically our highest level of training. That sounds a little backward, so let me explain.

If you set out to run thirty miles today, where do you think you'll easily get to without stopping? You'll get to your highest level of training. So if the most you've ever run comfortably is four miles, you'll peter out somewhere around there. Sure, adrenaline can take you a bit farther, and mind over matter is a big deal too; but typically your body will revert to what it knows and what it feels most comfortable with.

The same can be said for keeping promises to yourself.

If you decide on a goal—for example, "I'm going to write a novel" or "I'm going to run a 10K"—your subconscious will formulate the likelihood of that happening based on past experiences. So when it's day four and you're feeling tired and you don't want to head out for a run, you will revert to the highest level of mental training. What happened the last time you found yourself here? Did you push through and form a habit and get it done? Or did you make an excuse? Did you put it off until later?

Whatever standard you've set for yourself is where you'll end up . . . unless you fight through your instinct and change your pattern.

That's how I changed my own patterns and behaviors—how I established the rule in my life that I would no longer break a promise to myself no matter how small it was. It all began with Diet Coke.

I used to love—like, *obsessively* love—Diet Coke.

For the longest time I'd have several Diet Cokes a day. Then I realized how terrible they were for me. I cut my consumption down to one can a day, and I looked forward to that soda like an addict waiting for a high. *Do I want to drink it at lunchtime to give the afternoon a little pep? Or should I wait until dinner? We're eating Mexican food tonight, and Diet Coke is so good with chips and salsa, so maybe holding out is the right choice . . .*

I spent way too much time looking forward to the beverage. Then one summer I found myself with terrible vertigo, and I tried cutting anything out of my diet that might be harmful. Even my daily Diet Coke came into question.

Honestly, I thought to myself, *what kind of sicko gives up Diet Coke?! Are we supposed to just give up joy and goodness in our lives? Why don't I give up electricity and live like the Amish?*

My inner monologues are incredibly dramatic.

I decided to give it up for a month. I figured one month wasn't a long time . . . I could hold out for thirty days on anything. The only problem was, I'd never in my life successfully stuck to any kind of diet, exercise, writing, you-name-it without quitting or "cheating" at least a few times. What if just this once, though, I really saw it through?

And so I did.

For thirty days I didn't have any soda of any kind, which seems like no big deal when you're healthy and happy and not addicted. For me, that first week was a special kind of hell. *But what if,* I kept asking myself, *what if I just don't break this promise?* One day passed and then another, and by week three, it wasn't bad at all. At the end of the month I hadn't broken my word, and by then I didn't even crave DC anymore. It's been four years now, and it doesn't even occur to me to drink Diet Coke like I used to. When faced with it as an option, my instinct is to reach for my training—which tells me that I don't drink that stuff anymore. Establishing success in this one small area made me realize that the only thing standing between me and achieving my goals is the ability to build on past success.

Running my first half marathon? I got there by committing to running one mile a few times a week. When I kept that promise to myself, committing to running two miles a few times a week didn't seem like such a tough thing. My training told me that whatever goal I set I would keep, even if I was tired—so I kept showing up.

Writing my first book? It was the same kind of thing. Before that first completed manuscript, I'd started and stopped at least a dozen different novels. But once I got a first draft, I knew it was something I could do. When my instinct is to give up or walk away or throw my computer against the wall when I'm on a deadline, I remember how many times I've been here before. I used to wear the word count of my first novel on a cheap gold bracelet around my wrist: 82,311 was etched into it, and every time I looked at it, I would remember what I'd achieved. I was the one who'd strung 82,311 words together in semi-coherent sentences. When faced with the challenge of writing other books, I revert there . . . *Well,* I think, *at least I know I can write that many words. I've done it before!*

I know that blowing off a workout, a date, an afternoon to organize your closet, or some previous commitment to yourself doesn't seem like a big deal—but it is. It's a really big deal. Our words have power, but our actions shape our lives.

If you choose today not to break another promise to yourself, you will force yourself to slow down. You cannot keep every commitment, promise, goal, and idea without intentionality. If you recognize that your words have power and that your commitments carry covenant weight, you won't agree to anything so easily. You'll have to ask yourself if you really, truly have time to meet that friend for coffee this week. You'll have to decide if working out four times before Sunday is a real possibility, or if it's more realistic and achievable to commit to two beast-mode sessions and then one power walk with your neighbor.

You'll slow down and think things through.

You won't just talk about a goal; you'll plan for how you can meet it. You'll set a goal and surprise yourself when you achieve it. You'll teach yourself a new way to behave and set a standard for the type of person you truly are—not the one you've dreamed about becoming, but who you practice being every single day.

Also, maybe you'll consider giving up diet soda because the chemicals in that mess are terrible for you.

THINGS THAT HELPED ME . . .

1. *Starting with one small goal.* Diet Coke felt like my great white whale at the time, but in retrospect, giving up a soda was a million times easier than running marathons, hitting our annual budget goals, or writing a book. When someone tells me they want to start a diet, I'll suggest they start by aiming to drink half their body weight in ounces of water every day. It's much easier to add a habit than to take one away, but the water goal is a challenge. When they conquer that for the month, they've set a new standard for achievement and can add on something tougher.

2. *Being careful with my commitments.* We easily jump on board with anything that sounds good for us. A diet? Of course. Volunteering with church this Saturday? Absolutely. We know these things are important and good, so we say yes, assuming the value of the commitment will motivate us into following through. Unfortunately, that isn't always the case. Slow down your yes. Only commit to things you know you can accomplish because they're incredibly important to you. Otherwise you set yourself up for continued failure.

3. *Being honest with myself.* Be honest with yourself about what you're blowing off. A little cancellation here or a bow-out there can add up . . . but only if you refuse to acknowledge your actions. If you take a good hard look at what you've canceled on in the last thirty days, you might be shocked to discover how you're *training* yourself to behave.

CHAPTER 3

The lie:

I'M NOT GOOD ENOUGH

I am a workaholic.

And I don't say that lightly. The words are heavy; the knowledge makes my heart hurt. Though if I give myself a little grace, then the truth is I am a *recovering* workaholic.

I am a recovering workaholic, and I say those words with the same trepidation and shame that might exist were I to tell you that I had any other kind of addiction.

I looked up the definition just now, even though I've been certain of my diagnosis for a couple of years. My online dictionary app describes *workaholic* as "a person who feels compelled to work excessively."

Compelled.

That's a pretty strong word, isn't it? I can't be the only one who hears it and immediately thinks of *The Exorcist* and holy water and a terrified priest. But *compelled* feels accurate, like something inside of you that won't take no for an answer, like something you do without conscious thought.

Did I feel compelled to work nonstop?

Without question.

Even now I am typing this workaholic chapter at 5:37 in the morning because waking up to get my word count in at five o'clock is the only way I can actually manage to write books, run a media company, and raise a family at the same time. I still feel compelled to work until I'm exhausted, physically ill, pissed off at the world, or unable to focus my eyes—but at least they don't all happen at the same time anymore. I feel like I'm gaining on this problem.

Part of the reason I work so much is simple: I love my job. No, I *freaking* love my job. The people I work with are some of the kindest, coolest, most creative cats you'll ever meet. Each person on my team had to be vetted, and each role had to go through a couple of people before we got it right. Everyone had to be trained and had to train me right back on how to manage them and be a boss. I've spent years building this team. When I walk in and it's running well, when one person is creating the speaker lineup for our next live event, and someone else is taking the prettiest pictures you've ever seen, and the business team is booking new partnerships with some of the biggest brands on the planet, I feel proud. Proud to the very bottom of my toes that I—a high school graduate from the sticks—have put this together. Beyond that, my heart wants to burst because all of these people are working their butts off for *my* dream.

I had this fluffy, country-mouse idea that we could create a space on the internet that lifts up women from every walk of life, that makes them feel encouraged, that makes them feel like they have friends, that offers them help and advice and does it with positivity at all times. And you know what? It's totally working!

When I started blogging, only my mom and a few fiercely loyal aunts read the website. Now my digital reach is somewhere in the millions and climbing every day. My online tribe is awesome. I admire them, and on most days I think they admire me too—and I'm proud that I've created a business manifestation of my faith in action. Huzzah!

Then I go home.

At home, Sawyer is fighting with Ford over who gets which Lego piece. Jackson has a little attitude he picked up from someone at school, and if he rolls his eyes at me *one more time, Lord Jesus*, I'm going to rip off both his arms and whack him over the head with them. The baby is teething and fussy, and tomorrow is pajama day at preschool, but I'm going to miss it because I have a business trip. Dave and I are ships in the night, and we haven't had a date night in weeks—and yesterday I snapped at him over prepackaged lunches and then sobbed all over my pajamas because I felt like such a jerk. And, and, and . . . being a mom is hard work. I struggle with it all the time in a hundred different ways.

But being at work? Oh man, I have that in the bag! I excel at being at work. I am the Babe Ruth of knocking it out of the park in the lifestyle media sector!

So when given the choice between crushing it at the office or barely hanging on at home, I got in the habit of working, working, and working some more. Every time I succeeded in business, I counted it as validation that I was making the right choice.

But wait, folks. There's more . . .

You didn't think a major problem like this was caused by only one thing, did you? No way! Nobody's psychosis is one layer deep.

I am a Vidalia onion of issues. I've got a cartload of emotional baggage, so let's unpack some.

I am the baby of four children, and by the time my parents got around to my childhood, their marriage was deeply in trouble. Even though I was the youngest, I was a very self-sufficient child, and I think the combo of those two things meant that I was largely ignored—*unless* I did something good.

If I got an A on a test . . .

If I scored a goal in the soccer game . . .

If I got a part in the school play . . .

When I succeeded, I got praise and attention; I felt liked and accepted. But the moment the audience stopped clapping, it all went back to the way it was before.

What this taught me as a child—and what I carried into adulthood, as I discovered amid a load of therapy—is the belief that in order to be loved, I felt I needed to *produce* something.

Fast-forward to me in my thirties, and you'll see that it's nearly impossible for me to sit still. I am constantly moving and going and rushing through life. The second I achieve one goal, and I mean the second it's accomplished, I immediately think, *Okay, what next?* I struggle to celebrate or enjoy any victory, no matter how big, because I'm always mindful of something bigger I could be doing instead. At work I'm constantly at it. When I get home, I do dishes and organize cabinets and make a list of to-dos that will be impossible to accomplish in this lifetime or the next.

This need to prove my worth, coupled with the fact that I'm good at my career, made me one heck of a workaholic—yet I had no idea that I was one, or that my work was grievously affecting my health and the happiness of my family.

The very first time I had facial paralysis, I was nineteen years old. I was at the tail end of the first long, hard year with Dave, and

I knew the end was in sight. Not the end of the year—the end of our relationship altogether. He seemed more and more detached, and the long-distance relationship that we were trying so hard to make work just wouldn't. I could feel it coming—just like Phil Collins in that one song with the big drum solo—and I started to get anxious. I handled that anxiety the way I'd handled every other kind in my life: I doubled down at work. My already full plate became fuller. I wasn't even conscious of what I was trying to do; maybe I told myself that if I didn't stop to think about something bad happening, then it likely wouldn't.

One morning I woke up and noticed that my left eye was blinking half a second slower than my right. I assumed I was tired from work and wondered if I needed glasses. By the afternoon, my tongue started to tingle and then lost feeling completely. I went to the doctor, worried I might be having a stroke. That was the first time I'd ever heard of Bell's palsy. A quick Google search informed me that it was a *sometimes* temporary paralysis that causes damage to the nerves that control the movement of facial muscles. Within days I couldn't close my left eye, move my mouth, or feel anything on the left side of my face. I don't know why it's only one side of the face, but I can tell you, it only adds to the overall charm.

I had to wear an eye patch—which, by the way, is *super* sexy and basically every nineteen-year-old girl's dream. Because I couldn't move my lips, my speech was slurred and hard to understand. When I chewed I had to hold my mouth closed with my fingers for fear that food would fly out and kamikaze to the floor. The nerve damage causes neuralgia, which is also incredibly painful. During that time I felt so sorry for myself.

Even though it was fifteen years ago, I remember exactly how I felt when I looked in the mirror and realized how disfigured my face actually was. How I tried—in vain—to put on eyeliner or mascara, as if adding makeup would somehow make the paralysis go away. Or how each time I got the makeup on, I would inevitably cry it right back off. I spent those weeks perpetually worried, weighed down by the doctor's prognosis that this could last a few days or months on end. There was no way to be sure.

In retrospect, I never thought of myself as conceited. I never wore makeup or styled my hair until I was an adult, but having Bell's palsy made me hyperaware of the way I looked. I became completely depressed. I only got out of bed to go to work, and as soon as I got back home, I got back under the covers. I never wanted to leave my bed or even answer the phone. On the rare occasion that a friend talked me into leaving my apartment, I was mortified at the way people stared at me or pitied me when I tried to speak.

In the midst of it all, the bullet I had been trying to dodge found its mark. Dave broke up with me.

Okay, yes, breaking up with a girl with a paralyzed face was *not* his finest moment, and I feel the need to point out that sometimes we do stupid things that hurt our loved ones when we're trying to figure ourselves out. Since the moment we got back together, though (which happened when my face was still broken, by the way), he has been an incredible partner. The point is that I'd made myself severely ill trying to keep something inevitable from happening. When the palsy finally subsided a month later, I was beyond thankful, relieved that the worst was behind me. I chalked up the experience to a onetime bout of terrible luck.

A few years later Dave and I decided to take our first trip to Europe. This was back when we were child-free and could just dream up plans like, "What if we went to Europe?" With no babies or dogs or real responsibility, we just got ourselves a flight and toured old churches with our passports buried under our clothes for fear the "gypsies" we had heard about would rob us. God bless us.

When we made it to Florence, it was everything I dreamed Italy would be. We ate loads of pasta, walked the cobblestone streets, and made out like it was our part-time job. We spent whole afternoons imagining our future and what we would name our unborn dream children. It was one of the most romantic experiences of my life.

By the time we got to Venice a few days later, my tongue had started to go numb.

I stood in an Italian hotel room and sobbed because I knew the palsy had come back. Our beautiful vacation was now being marred by the stress of trying to get medical help in another country. As an aside, using my English-to-Italian translation guidebook to explain to a Venetian pharmacist that I needed an eye patch is still one of the most comical experiences of my life! Also, the eye patch—plus my paralyzed face—meant that we got to go to the front of every line in customs. Silver lining.

Ever the comedians, Dave and I made jokes about the assets of such an illness. For example, I did an *amazing* Sammy Davis Jr. impersonation! Also, the pirate jokes were endless. Yar! It wasn't until we arrived in Paris—a lifelong dream destination of mine—that even jokes couldn't lift my spirits. As we walked through the Champ de Mars, I realized the photo I had always dreamed of—me in front of the Eiffel Tower—would forever be a reminder of this illness. As much as I hate to admit it, I've never felt sorrier for myself than in that moment. In that old photograph (which you can Google, by the way, because I'm not afraid to share any pic on the internet, apparently), I'm standing alone in front of the tower, bundled up for the weather. I'm wearing sunglasses to try and hide the eye patch, and since a smile would have only worked on one half of my face, I just did nothing at all.

When we got back home, the doctor put me on steroids and sent me to see a neurologist to make sure the palsy wasn't a symptom of something greater. After the doctors didn't find the brain tumor I was sure was there, they gave me an interesting prognosis. Both times I'd gotten palsy I'd been under extreme stress. Like many women, I was working so hard and not taking good care of myself. I argued that this couldn't be the case. After all, I'd gotten sick again while on a romantic vacation. That's when Dave pointed out that it was the first vacation we'd taken in three years. Three years of sixty-hour weeks followed by one two-week break does not a decompressed girl make. I was also at the beginning of launching a business, and I was staying busy, desperate to prove myself. We were trying to get pregnant at the time, and though I was only twenty-four, month after month after month had passed by without a baby. Rather than managing that stress, I had just given myself more things to do.

Our bodies are incredible. They can do unbelievable things. They will also tell you exactly what they need if you're willing to listen. And if you're not, if you try to do too many things without rest, they will absolutely shut down to get what they need.

About three years ago I started to develop symptoms of vertigo. I'd stand up at work, and the room would sway around me. I felt dizzy throughout the day, my eyes had trouble focusing, and I spent most of my time feeling nauseous. For weeks I assumed I must need more sleep, more water, or less Diet Coke. When it got so bad I was afraid to drive with my kids in the car, I decided to see a doctor.

I saw so many doctors.

Internists, allergists, ENTs . . . Nobody could quite figure it out. I ate well. I was healthy. I ran marathons, for goodness' sakes. They all agreed I had vertigo but couldn't definitively tell me why.

Eventually the ENT suggested it was seasonal vertigo brought on by my allergies, and since no one else had a better idea, I went with it. "Take an allergy pill every day," he told me. So I did.

Every night, without fail, I took my pill. Sometimes when the spinning got really bad, I took a second one, which made me crazy drowsy, but at least it calmed the vertigo. I did this for over a year and resigned myself to the fact that life would be a little dizzier forever. It wasn't a big deal, I told myself. It only meant that instead of giving 100 percent, I now would need to give 130 percent to make up for not being able to work as fast anymore. It sounds crazy to write that, but in my overachieving mind, it made absolute sense.

Then, about two years ago, I heard about a homeopathic doctor who specialized in vertigo. I'd never gone to a homeopathic doctor in my life, but at that point if someone had said I could cure my constant nausea with voodoo and the sacrifice of a spring chicken, I would have seriously considered it.

I went to meet with him, his ponytail, his shirt made of organic hemp, and his life-sized statue of Ganesh, and I tried to keep an open mind while he talked into the air beside him instead of to me. I laid out the whole story of when I got sick and how it affected me, and he asked a hundred questions about my emotions, my childhood, and the deeper reasons why I felt a certain way. I kept thinking, *When is he going to prescribe some medicine? Why are we still talking about stress?* And, *What's the deal with that little collection of crystals?* Before I'd gone to him I assumed homeopathic doctors tell you to stop your sugar intake, or, God forbid, stop eating dairy because it messes with your chakras or whatever.

But after two hours of me talking, he abruptly interrupted and announced to the room, "No more. I know what's wrong!"

Then he blew me away. He pointed out that my vertigo had

come on for the first time when I was under extreme stress at work. And every time it got so bad that I couldn't even lift my head off a pillow? It was because the stress had gotten worse.

That time I had a big turnover of staff at Chic? Vertigo. That time I was so excited to write my first contracted book but then was positive it was terrible and I'd be fired and have to pay back the advance? Vertigo. In every single instance, my vertigo was a physical response to an emotional problem. *A physical response to an emotional problem.*

I didn't even know our bodies did that!

Okay, I knew it in the same way that every other God-fearing, law-abiding woman who watched Oprah and heard about self-care knows it, but I grew up in the country. I got a shotgun for my thirteenth birthday. I may have lived in LA for fourteen years, but my rub-some-dirt-on-it tendencies run deep. His words hit me like ice water, and now that I knew he was right, I immediately wanted to know how to fix it and get back to normal.

"Go home and do nothing," he told me.

"I'm sorry, what?"

"Go home and do nothing. Sit around, watch TV, spend an entire day on the sofa. Discover that your world doesn't implode without you going a hundred miles an hour. Get up the next day and do it again."

Verily I say unto you, dear reader, his words made me want to throw up. It sounds crazy—it *is* kind of crazy—but the idea of doing nothing makes my skin crawl. Even when I'm at home I'm constantly doing something. If I'm not taking care of the kids, I'm organizing the house, cleaning out my closet, or giving myself a DIY facial.

"What would happen to you if you stopped moving?" he asked me.

I shook my head in blind panic. The image of a shark floating to the surface of the ocean, dead from lack of movement, came to mind.

All I could think was, *I don't know, but it will be bad.*

Talk about life-altering moments. Talk about someone holding a mirror up to your face and making you realize you're not actually the person you think you are at all. I spent my days thinking up ways to help women live a better life, and the whole time I truly believed I was qualified to teach it because I was actually living it. Meanwhile, I wasn't doing the most fundamental thing a woman needs to do before she can take care of anyone else: take care of herself!

I needed a drastic life change.

I forced myself to stop working so many hours. I went to the office from nine thirty to four thirty and was shocked to discover that the world continued to spin on its axis. I pushed myself to rest, to sit and do nothing. It gave me massive anxiety, so I poured myself a glass of wine and kept right on sitting there. I started volunteering at the local homeless shelter. I took a hip-hop dance class. Turns out, I'm terrible at hip-hop dance class, but I love it so much I laugh like a toddler through the entire hour-long process. I looked for joy. I looked for peace.

I stopped drinking so much caffeine. I played with my kids. I did a lot of therapy. And then I did some more. I prayed. I looked up every scripture in the Bible that talks about rest. I had dinner with my girlfriends. I went on dates with my husband. I taught myself to take it one day at a time, to stop obsessing over the next victory, and to appreciate the simple parts of today. I learned to celebrate accomplishments, not with big flashy parties, but with taco nights or a great bottle of wine.

I acknowledged my own hard work and the achievements of

my company, and I learned to rest in the knowledge that I will still be okay even if both of those things go away tomorrow. I studied the gospel and finally grasped the divine knowledge that I am loved and worthy and enough . . . as I am.

Learning to rest is an ongoing process. Like any other lifelong behavior, I constantly fight the desire to slip back into the role I've played for so long. They say the first step is admitting you have a problem, and two years ago I did just that. I learned that I am a recovering workaholic, but through this process, I also learned that I am a child of God—and that trumps everything else.

THINGS THAT HELPED ME . . .

1. *I went to therapy.* This could be the first thing I list for every single element I've worked through, but it's especially real in this case. Were it not for my therapist, I never would have understood the connection between my childhood insecurities and my adult accomplishments. Were it not for my therapist, I never would have realized that the drive for accomplishment can actually be harmful. I cannot recommend therapy enough, and if I had Beyoncé's money, the first thing I'd do is pay for therapy for every woman I could find. Ask your friends to recommend someone they like, or ask your gynecologist to refer you. A doctor for your lady parts knows the right kind of counselor for a woman. Trust me.

2. *I hustled for joy.* Work just as hard for fun moments, vacation moments, and pee-your-pants-laughing moments as you do for all the other things. I encourage you to take a walk, call a friend, have a glass of wine, enjoy a bubble bath, or take a long lunch. All of that work will be there when you get back, and a

little time away can recharge your batteries and give you the energy to battle that ever-growing to-do list.

3. *I reordered my list.* When I ask most women to name the things on their priority list, they can throw them out there no problem: kids, partner, work, faith, etc. The order may change, but the bullet points rarely do. You know what also rarely changes no matter how many women I talk to? Women actually putting *themselves* on their own priority list. You should be the very first of your priorities! Are you getting enough sleep, enough water, the right nutrition? You cannot take care of others well if you're not first taking care of yourself. Also, one of the best ways to ensure that you stop trying to run from your problems is to face them head-on.

CHAPTER 4

The Lie:

I'M BETTER THAN YOU

I feel the need to confess . . . I shave my toes.

I totally do.

Sometimes—not all the time, mind you—I look down in the shower and see my big toes sporting locks long enough to braid. It's embarrassing, sure, but a quick swipe of my razor returns my toe knuckles to their usual silky-smooth glory.

None of this would be such an epic admission for me to make except that I once made fun of a girl in freshman-year English class for doing this exact thing. *Blargh!* I feel like such a jerk even now, a hundred and fifty years later.

Friends, let me paint a quick picture of myself in high school. I was a solid twenty pounds heavier, I wore clothes from Goodwill, and I was the president of the drama club. I wasn't someone who teased others; I was someone who *got* teased. But there was that one instance when I did tease—the one and only time in my memory that I actively made fun of someone else. Maybe that's why it sticks out in my brain. Maybe that's why it still feels so shameful.

We'll call this girl Schmina.

Her actual name is Tina, but I'm trying to write in code here.

Schmina was the girl who always seemed totally confident in herself. She developed breasts and a sense of humor light-years before the rest of us, and she was popular in a way I would never be. One day in Mrs. Jachetti's English class, when we were supposed to be writing a paper on Zora Neale Hurston, Schmina mentioned something about shaving her toes. I don't know why she mentioned it . . . I assume popular girls share grooming tidbits the way the rest of us mortals talk about the weather. But anyway, while I didn't say anything to her directly, I talked soooo much smack about it to my best friend later that day. "Who shaves their feet? More importantly, who has hairy digits in need of shaving? Schmina clearly has some kind of glandular disease she's not copping to."

What a ridiculous conversation! Most people would have forgotten about a conversation like that by now, but it keeps haunting me years later because the whole time I was mocking Schmina and her hairy toes, *I was totally shaving my own!* To this day, hand to God, whenever I look down at my big toe and see that it's looking a little shaggy, I think about what a jerk my teenage self was.

Rach flaw number one? Hairy digits.

Rach flaw number two? Hypocrisy.

A story about hairy toes, a girl named Schmina, and the adolescent angst I really should have worked through with a licensed therapist years ago may seem like the most frivolous topic ever. But then, I daresay that tearing down other women is usually based on something no less frivolous than the insecurities of our fourteen-year-old selves.

Why do we do it, ladies? Why do we gossip? Why do we rag on each other? Why do we say hello on Sunday mornings with the same tongues we use to lash others behind their backs a few days later? Does it make us feel better about ourselves? Does it make us feel safer to mock someone who has stepped outside of the parameters we deem acceptable? If we can point out their flaws, does doing so diminish our own?

Of course it doesn't. In fact, the stones we most often try and fling at others are the ones that have been thrown at us.

Have you ever shaved your toes?

And what I really mean by that is, have you ever made fun of someone else? Have you ever pointed your finger in their direction and ignored the three other fingers on your hand pointing back at you? We've all been there, but that doesn't make it okay. Bringing others down won't elevate you. Recognizing that all words have power—even the ones whispered behind someone's back—is how you adjust your behavior.

A few weeks ago there was a woman on my plane from LA to Chicago. She and her husband were traveling with two boys, the youngest of whom was about four. He was also the worst-behaved child I've ever seen. Before we'd even pulled back from the gate, he was screaming—and I don't mean a whine or a protest. I mean screaming bloody murder about having to sit in a seat when he wanted to run around. His mother had to forcibly hold him in the chair for at least half an hour while he hollered to be released. Everyone on the plane, myself included, was miserable until he stopped. But a little while later, when I got up to go to the restroom, I saw why he'd finally quieted: he'd been given a big bag of gummy worms to happily eat his way through.

Friends, I will be honest with you. I was disgusted.

First of all, as a strict parent who was raised by strict parents, listening to him screaming, I thought, *Oh, heck no!* All through takeoff I was thinking about his mom. I was thinking about how she needed to discipline him better, have boundaries, get support from her spouse. And when I saw that she'd rewarded his bad behavior? And with *sugar*? Keep me near the cross, Lord Jesus! I kept thinking, *This woman doesn't have a clue.*

Later at the baggage claim, I saw the family again. The four-year-old was wild—jumping up on a stopped luggage belt, hitting his brother, and running around in circles while everyone stared. *What is wrong with his mother?* I kept thinking, *Why doesn't she get a handle on him?!*

Then I saw her standing next to the luggage carousel . . . utterly exhausted. When I *really* looked at her, I saw she was near tears, looking bewildered and totally overwhelmed. Her husband wore the same shell-shocked expression as their son ran in circles around them.

And a gentle voice reminded me, *Rachel, you don't know their story.*

I was so humbled in my ignorance. Maybe this little boy had special needs that made it hard for him to control his impulses. Maybe this little boy was a new adoptive child who had struggled in foster homes for most of his young life—something I should be graceful about, given what we've been through. Maybe this little boy was just badly behaved and his parents were struggling to discipline him because their older son had been easy to manage at this age. Whatever the reason, I will never know—because instead of asking or offering the benefit of the doubt, I cast my judgment on her before I even asked myself why things might be this way.

Women judging other women. It's been on my heart for a while. It's something I've tried to wrap my brain around fully so I could put it into words. I see it all around me in so many different ways, and that poor, tired mama on the flight to Chicago reminded me of what I want to say.

What I want to say is that we all judge each other, but even though we all do it, that's not an excuse. Judging is still one of the most hurtful, spiteful impulses we own, and our judgments keep us from building a stronger tribe . . . or from having a tribe in the first place. Our judgment prohibits us from beautiful, life-affirming friendships. Our judgment keeps us from connecting in deeper, richer ways because we're too stuck on the surface-level assumptions we've made.

Ladies, our judging has to stop.

So does our compulsion to compete with everyone around us.

Let me give an example of that too. When I heard that some of my girlfriends were going to run the Nike Women's Half Marathon in San Francisco, I was excited. For some of them, it was their first race. I was also overjoyed because it would involve a weekend trip somewhere. I promptly invited myself along for the ride. The plan was for us to leave on Friday, drive the five-ish hours between LA and SF, hang out in town on Saturday, then run the race and drive home on Sunday. Wait. Scratch that. *They* would run the race . . . I would stand on the side of the road and clap for them while they jogged by. This felt especially interesting because I am a runner . . . and more than that, I am competitive about running. I like to challenge myself. I like to try bigger and better races. I like to beat my personal record and push myself to be the best. What I *do not like*—what I had never actually done—is cheering for others while they do something I am fully capable of doing right along with them. I kept thinking, *What if I didn't need to prove myself in this situation? What if making myself into someone better has more to do with my willingness to be of service than my willingness to compete?*

So I went to San Francisco. In fact, I *drove everyone* to San Francisco because I figured the last thing I'd want if I were about to run thirteen miles would be to drive four hundred miles.

It's worth saying that while I did all of this and had so much stinking fun with the ladies, I didn't always have a good attitude about my willingness to be a cheerleader. On Sunday morning when everyone headed out bright and early to the starting line, I got myself together and headed in the other direction, to the five-mile marker. About twenty minutes into my journey, I realized it was unlikely that I would get a cab at six a.m. on a Sunday morning. Around this time I realized that walking alone in the dark in downtown SF might be one of the dumbest things I've ever done. I legitimately thought at one point, *See, this is what happens when you try and do something nice: you get murdered on the streets of an unknown city!*

I get pretty dramatic when I am in fear for my life and haven't had any coffee.

Anyway, at that point I decided to turn around and head for the finish line since walking there felt safer than walking to mile five. Turns out, walking to the finish line meant walking up approximately thirty-two hills that were taller than some mountains I know. I was sweaty and grouchy by the time I arrived, grumbling under my breath about the whole ordeal, and thinking, *Why on earth did I agree to do this?*

Then I saw my first elite marathon runner.

Elite marathon runners are those superhumans who run a race in like five minutes. They look like cheetahs or gazelles as they fly down the road, and they are truly breathtaking to behold.

As someone who ran twelve-and-a-half-minute miles in my first marathon (elite female runners, by comparison, run like six- or seven-minute miles), I was in awe. Since I'm always so far behind these athletes in the race, I've never been able to see one. I stood there and watched one after another sprint by and felt so blessed to see them in action. For the two and a half hours that followed, I stood in that exact spot and cheered on strangers. I clapped non-stop (my skill as a preacher's daughter finally coming into play!). I screamed until my throat was sore. I yelled all the things that encourage me when I hear them from the sidelines during a race.

"You are so strong!"

"You're almost there!"

"You can do this!"

And the last one is something I've never heard but always tell myself when it gets hard during a run. I yelled it over and over again whenever I saw someone who looked ready to drop:

"You've lived through tougher things than this. Don't give up now!"

Finally, it was there in that exact spot that I got to see my friends Katie and Brittany jogging up from mile twelve in their first-ever half marathon. You can see it in a picture someone shot of us. I'm screaming like a maniac and trying not to throw myself over the fence to attack them with hugs. I was so proud of them I was laughing and crying—as if their achievement was somehow my own. I jogged alongside them, outside the track, wrapped up in the joy of the moment, and I heard God very distinctly say, "Imagine all of the things you would have missed today if you'd only been out here for yourself."

I never would have seen the elite runners. I never would have been there when my friend Hannah ran her personal best (13.1 miles in under two hours!). I wouldn't have been able to stand next to Joy, who put my cheering to shame. After running her own race, she screamed louder than anyone from the sidelines, encouraging the other runners. I wouldn't have been there to hug Katie and Brittany. I wouldn't have seen any of it . . . I would have run another half marathon, like I'd done ten times before, and I'd have had nothing to show for it but a little extra pride and the banana they give you at the end.

The first step toward getting past the desire to judge and compete is admitting that nobody is immune. For some of us, we judge in little ways: rolling our eyes at the way someone is dressed, frowning at a badly behaved child in the grocery store, or making assumptions about another mother at school pickup who has a serious expression and wears a suit every day and seems uptight. For others, judging is a bigger problem: berating your little sister because her views are different from yours, viciously gossiping with other women, taking to social media to write hateful things to people you don't even know simply because they've stepped outside the lines of what you think is good.

The second step is recognizing that just because you believe it doesn't mean it's true for everyone. In so many instances judgment comes from a place of feeling as though you've somehow got it all figured out when they do not. Judging each other actually makes us feel safer in our own choices. Faith is one of the most abused instances of this. We decide that our religion is right; therefore, every other religion must be wrong. Within the same religion, or heck, even within the same church, people judge each other for not being the right kind of Christian, Catholic, Mormon, or Jedi. I don't know the central tenet of your faith, but the central tenet of mine is "love thy neighbor." Not "love thy neighbor if they look and act and think like you." Not "love thy neighbor so long as they wear the right clothes and say the right things."

Just love them.

Yes, I also believe in holding each other accountable; but holding each other accountable takes place inside community and relationships. Holding each other accountable comes from a beautiful place in the heart of friendship that makes you sit down with your friend and ask with love if they've looked at their own actions in a particular light. Holding each other accountable comes from a place of love. Judgment comes from a place of fear, disdain, or even hate. So be careful about dressing your judgments up as accountability to make your conscience feel better.

I have worked tirelessly over the last couple of years to create content that caters to women. I have spent numerous hours trying to figure out exactly what women like us want in life. Do you know what they want? Do you know the number one thing that I hear most, get emails about most, get asked for advice on most? Friends. How to make friends. How to keep friends. How to cultivate real, valuable relationships. That's what women are craving. That's what they really want and hope for, and if that's true, we have to start at the beginning.

We start from the beginning, and we teach ourselves to keep an open mind. We begin with that first hello or handshake, and we stop ourselves from making decisions not founded in fact and experience. We look for commonality instead of seeking out differences. We ignore things like hair or clothes or weight or race or religion or socioeconomic background. We pay attention to things like character and heart and wisdom and experience. And no, it might not be easy, but I promise it will be worth it. Your tribe is out there, and if you haven't found it yet, I'd challenge you to consider that maybe your people come in a different package than you thought they might.

41

THINGS THAT HELPED ME . . .

1. *Nonjudgmental friends.* We often become whomever we surround ourselves with. If your friends are full of gossip and vitriol, I promise you'll start to develop the habit. When you're looking for a community of women, look for the ones who want to build each other up instead of tear each other down.

2. *Policing myself.* If we're already judgmental (and let's be honest, most of us are), we have to work hard on policing ourselves. When I find myself judging someone in my head, I force myself to stop and think of compliments about that person. By doing this, I'm learning to look for the positive instead of reaching for the negatives.

3. *Dealing with it.* Usually our judgment and gossip come from a deep well of our own insecurities. Get to the bottom of what's going on with *you.* What's making you lash out at others? The first step toward becoming the best version of yourself is being honest, truly honest, about what makes you tick.

CHAPTER 5

The lie:

LOVING HIM IS ENOUGH FOR ME

I fell in love the first time I saw him.

Does that sound dramatic? Probably. I'm not even sure I was aware of it at the time, but the scene plays out so clearly in my memory.

I went out to the lobby to get my boss's eleven o'clock appointment. There was only one man standing there. His back was to me, hands down deep in his pockets. He had a beat-up leather messenger bag slung over his shoulder.

I noticed the bag first.

I remember thinking it was so cool that this guy wore business clothes but carried a worn-in leather bag instead of a briefcase.

"Excuse me," I said as I crossed the lobby. "Are you here to meet with Kevin?"

In my mind, he turns around in slow motion. The memory illuminates when I first see his face. He smiles at me and reaches out a hand to shake mine. The moment stretches into infinity, then snaps back together like elastic. It speeds back up into real time.

Something just happened, I distinctly remember thinking. I was equal parts excited and terrified. He was older and totally out of my league. Still, I caught myself thinking, *But maybe . . .*

That maybe is what did it. My curiosity wouldn't go away. It was enough to startle me, to make me wish I was wearing something cuter than a black maxi skirt and an ill-fitting matching T-shirt.

That day wasn't the first time I'd spoken to him; he called to talk to my boss often. It was the first time I'd spoken to him in person. I'd had no idea what he looked like, or more specifically, that he was so handsome—and what *had* been a business relationship quickly turned into something more flirtatious.

It's important to note here that I had *zero* experience with men. I'd been hired as an intern during my first year of college. That summer they offered me a job, and I promptly dropped out of school to accept it. I had just turned nineteen years old. At this ripe old age, I had smooched a couple of boys in high school, but I'd never had a real relationship and had never been on a date. I might have been professionally mature beyond my years, but when it came to romance, I had the life experience of an amoeba.

Our relationship progressed over email and staring at each other during business functions. It's probably also fair to tell you that I had my big sister's ID, so at those business functions I ordered a glass of wine like everyone else. Given the job I had, this man never thought to question my age. I also never willingly volunteered the information.

It's also worth telling you that he was eight years and a lifetime of experience ahead of me.

He asked me out on my first real date, and I spent days trying to figure out what to wear. I was a little surprised to find him dressed so casually when I arrived. It was telling, in retrospect—his preparation for this date versus mine—but I can only see that in hindsight.

We walked down the street to a little Italian restaurant. I tried to keep it cool, though internally I was freaking out that we were *on a date!* I was so nervous. I worried that he would try to hold my hand or kiss me, or both! I had no idea how to handle either situation with grace, and I prayed fervently that I wouldn't be put into a position to figure it out.

We were seated at a table. We ordered a bottle of wine.

"I hope you're not one of those girls who's afraid to eat on a date." He laughed.

It annoyed me. Whoever or whatever kind of girl I was hadn't been determined yet. I didn't like the comparison to anyone else, didn't like the reminder that this wasn't his very first date too.

I responded by eating more than half the pizza we were sharing. He talked about himself for two hours straight. I didn't mind. I was fascinated.

That night when he walked me to my car, I thought I might be sick. I was 99 percent sure he would try to kiss me, and I felt confident that I wasn't a girl who kissed on the first date. I mean, I had no practice with this theory, but it felt like the truth. So when I went to throw my bag into the front seat and turned around to see him leaning in, I immediately threw both hands up in between us—real graceful like—and yelled, "Don't kiss me!"

He paused, a deer in headlights, before chuckling like some sexy leading man.

"I was going to give you a hug," he told me. He reached for my hand and gave it a firm shake. "But just to be safe."

It was so charming I wanted to die. My mortification knew no bounds. I drove away from that date bemused and a little bit in love. I was positive, beyond a shadow of a doubt, that I would marry that man.

After one meal of pizza and cheap red wine, we were officially dating . . . or at least, I thought we were.

I didn't know there were rules.

I didn't know there was even a game.

Soon after that first date, he asked me out on another. This time for soup at an ultra-hip restaurant that was popular at the time. Only in LA can you unironically invite someone on a date to the trendy local soup joint and nobody finds it odd.

A week later he asked me when I'd graduated college—because, dude, I still hadn't told him my age. On some level I knew he wasn't going to be happy about our age difference. The email I wrote him back (because this was before text messaging, kids) started with, *Well, this should be interesting . . .*

He responded like a champ. He told me I was Doogie Howser, and I *did* feel like some sort of child prodigy, because not only did I have this job but also I was in a real relationship with a grown-up. I didn't know it at the time, but on the other side of that email, that *grown-up* was very unhappy.

It came up on our next date: I was too young, I was too inexperienced in every way, and he didn't want to be the guy that hurt me.

Can you believe me when I tell you that I didn't hear him at all? I mean, my ears were working just fine, but my brain couldn't even process the idea. I kept thinking, *How in the world could you possibly hurt me? We're going to get married and have babies, and it's going to be awesome!*

I mean . . . bless my tiny, ignorant heart.

He resisted, but I was dogged in my pursuit. I thought I was mature enough to handle it. I went quickly from never having gone on a date to spending every night at his apartment. For clarity's sake, let me spell it out: at that point we weren't having sex . . . but honestly, that was a technicality.

Are you supposed to admit all of this when you write a book for a Christian publisher? I have no idea. But I know for a fact that I am not the only "good Christian girl" who fell in love with a man and threw every ideal she'd ever believed right out the window because nothing mattered to her more than being loved by him.

A month into our relationship we went to a party at my friend's house, and because I was a tiny baby bunny, I introduced everyone to my boyfriend that night.

"This is my boyfriend. Have you met my boyfriend? Who's he? Oh, that's just my *boyfriend!*"

Oh, I cringe at the memory. I also cringe remembering the next day, when he was clearly upset with me but wouldn't tell me why. I kept asking until he finally gave a frustrated huff. "You've never acted your age before, but last night it was like it was written on your shirt."

Ouch.

On the one hand, in a lot of ways, he was right. I had always been incredibly professional at work and mature when we hung out, but in this instance I didn't know the rules. I didn't understand that you couldn't just call a guy your boyfriend without a discussion. I naïvely believed that if someone had seen your boobs and you regularly went to dinner together, it meant you were a couple. Just to put a little more truth on this, I had zero guilt about the whole *here are my boobs* thing because I believed we were getting married. I justified my choices because I thought they were part of the bigger story of us. Meanwhile, this man didn't even believe we were *dating*.

Thirty-four-year-old Rachel can see all of this so clearly in hindsight. Nineteen-year-old me was in love and insecure, so I justified everything he said or did that was hurtful.

It's hard for me to write all of this down. It will be hard for my husband to read it. Dave is so different from that man, and it will be tough for him to learn—in detail I've never fully shared—how much this treatment hurt me.

But here's the deal: I am not the only woman who ever let a man treat her badly. It's important to tell my story because I believe some of you may find yourself in a similar situation now. And just like me, you're maybe so deeply inside the forest you can't see the trees. In telling my story and my truth, I hope it can help some of you make better choices than I did, or see your reality for what it actually is.

Because here's the ugly truth: I was a booty call.

The preacher's daughter, the one who hadn't ever been on a date, the conservative good girl . . . *I* drove to this man's house every single night he asked me to and pretended that it didn't gut me when he wouldn't acknowledge me during the day.

When we were together, he was so sweet and so loving that it held me over during the times when he wouldn't call. On the rare occasions when I'd meet up with him at a bar and his friends would ignore me—or worse—refer to me only as "the nineteen-year-old" and he wouldn't say anything to stop them, I made excuses. I was like the overweight girl at school who makes fun of herself before anyone else can . . . I acted as though I was in on the joke, that *I was a joke*—that I wasn't worth defending. When he would flirt with other girls in front of me or invite me somewhere just to ignore me all night, I told myself to play it cool. He'd reacted so badly when I called him my boyfriend, and I'd learned enough to know that if I brought up any of this I'd be seen as clingy. I took whatever scraps he gave me, and worse still, I was *thrilled* to receive them.

As I write these words, I'm crying.

I didn't cry when I wrote the chapter about my brother's death or the pain of my childhood—but this? This flays me. I am so sad for that little girl who didn't know better. I am devastated that nobody prepared her for life or taught her to love herself so she wasn't so desperate to get any form of it from someone else. I'm sad that she had to figure it out on her own. I'm disappointed that it took her so long.

It took me a year—a whole year of *whatever you want, whatever you need, whatever you think is best*—a year during which I tried *everything* I could think of, tried to *be* everything he wanted. Attentive but not clingy. Pretty without trying too hard. Funny and smart and cool. Nice to his friends even when they treated me like garbage. Caring and thoughtful when he wanted me around, and never bothering him if he didn't call me first. Toward the end of that year, when his company moved him to another state and our already tenuous relationship was threatened, my virginity went from technical to nonexistent. It was the last, best way I could think of to hold on to him.

It didn't work.

Two months after he moved away, he flew home long enough to break up with me.

He wanted a clean break, he said. He needed a chance to really put down roots in his new city, he said. He cared about me, he said. It just wasn't going to work out, he said. We'd always be friends, he said.

I can see it perfectly in my mind, though I don't often remember that day in real detail because it was so heartbreaking for me. My bed had a bright pink and orange Ikea comforter, and as I sat in the middle of it, I wept. The memory makes me lower my head, and it brings my heart to its knees. You may read this chapter and feel anger at the way that man treated me, or anger at the position I'd put myself in—but I didn't see any of it.

I had no pride.

I sat in the middle of that neon duvet, and instead of standing up for myself, I begged him not to leave me.

He left anyway.

I cried myself to sleep that night.

The next morning I got in my car and drove to my hometown two hours away to spend Thanksgiving with my family. That day was miserable. Use your imagination to dream up the kind of conversations I was forced into by well-meaning Southern aunts when I'd been dumped.

Jesus wept.

When I got back in my car to drive home that night, I saw that I had a voicemail. Somehow I knew he'd call me that day—it was routine, after all. He would do something hurtful, then I would accept it and wait by the phone to see if he wanted another go.

I held off listening to that call for the two hours it took me to get back to my apartment. I dialed the number for my voice-mail and stood immobile as I listened to his message. He was just checking on me, he said, wanted to make sure I was okay.

It was a divine moment in my life. Never before or since have I experienced such total clarity. I stood in my crappy Hollywood apartment and saw our relationship like a map before me. There was the spot where we first kissed. The detour when we didn't talk for two weeks after I called him my boyfriend. The night he flirted with the popular girls from work in front of me. Then there was the day I first heard the line: "We're not together, but we're not *not* together." I saw that phrase and platitudes like it scattered like mortar shells over the terrain. There was the first time he called and asked me to come over after getting drunk at a bar I wasn't invited to.

For a year I'd only looked at the pretty parts of our relationship, and for the first time I made myself see what was really there.

"Who are you?" I asked my empty bedroom.

But that was the wrong question to ask. The issue wasn't that I didn't know who I was; the problem was that I didn't know who I had allowed myself to become.

It might surprise you to know that I don't blame him for anything that happened that year. Though he was a grown man, he had his own baggage. He was young and immature in his own way. People will treat you with as much or as little respect as you allow them to, and our dysfunctional relationship started the first time he treated me badly and I accepted it.

I called him back, just as I had a hundred times before. But this time I was totally calm. I had no anxiety about what he might think, and I wasn't excited to talk to him. When he answered the phone, he immediately launched into questions about how I was feeling and if I'd had fun with my family—as if we were old friends catching up, as if he hadn't eviscerated me the day before.

"Hey," I interrupted him.

He went silent. I like to believe there was something in my tone that made him pause, but perhaps it was simply startling because I'd never interrupted before.

Calmly and without any dramatics, I told him, "I am done with this. I am done with you. Don't ever call me again."

It wasn't a bid for attention or an attempt at playing hard to get; I meant every single word.

"Why?" he choked out.

"Because I don't deserve to be treated like this. Because I can't go back and forth. Because I don't like what I've become . . . but mostly because you said we were friends. This whole time, whatever else has happened, you told me I was your friend. I don't want to be friends if this is how you treat someone you care about."

I meant those words with every fiber of my being. I hung up on him and shut off my phone. I brushed my teeth and put on pajamas. Then I went to bed and crawled under that pink blanket and went to sleep dry-eyed and peaceful for the first time in months. I remember that night as the first time I really felt like a grown woman.

I woke up to someone banging on my front door.

This is the great part of the story. This is the moment that feels like a movie or a romance novel.

This is where I tell you that I woke up and found my husband on the other side of my front step.

The man who treated me badly, who had strung me along, and who couldn't make up his mind was lost somewhere between his parents' house and my apartment that Thanksgiving night. I know it seems dramatic, but that's really what happened. I remember everything in our relationship as either *before* or *after* this moment: our love story being reborn.

And it is a love story. Our relationship is the greatest gift in my life. Dave is my best friend, the first real caretaker I ever had, and I have had the honor of watching him grow from that guy into a wonderful husband, father, and friend.

But every story is not perfect.

Very few roads to love are easy to navigate, and ours was no exception. But it's important to me that you know that while our journey hasn't been easy, the fourteen years since that first really crappy one have totally outweighed the mistakes we both made. It's important for me to tell this story because it is the story of us. My husband is brave and humble to support me in sending it out in the world in hopes that it might serve someone else. It's also important to understand that I don't believe this is typically how it works out.

Opening the door that night and finding Dave on the front porch begging me for one more chance feels special because it was special. What is far more likely to happen in most cases is that as long as you allow someone to treat you badly, they will continue to do so. If you're not able to value yourself, no one else will either. I hesitate to even tell you the ending because I don't want anyone to use it as an excuse to stay in an unhealthy relationship in hopes that it will become healthy. Our story ended well, but that wouldn't have happened if I hadn't been willing to walk away. That night in my bedroom, I hit the point where I couldn't live one more day without self-respect; I couldn't stay with a partner who didn't truly value who I was as a person. Sometimes choosing to walk away, even if it means breaking your own heart, can be the greatest act of self-love you have access to.

What else can I tell you? What can I offer you as insight or wisdom or what I hope you receive from this chapter? I hope that if you read yourself in my story, it will hold up a mirror for you. I hope you'll get out of the trees long enough to see the forest for what it is. I hope that those of you who've lived through something similar and carry guilt about it long after it's over will learn that you are not the only one.

So many women have made mistakes or done things they regret or become versions of themselves they aren't happy with. So many other women have survived and come out the other side stronger because of it. Every day you're choosing who you are and what you believe about yourself, and you're setting the standards for the relationships in your life. Every day is a chance to start over.

THINGS THAT (WOULD HAVE) HELPED ME . . .

1. *A sounding board.* When I walked through this season, I didn't really have any close friends or mentors who could advise me. I think if I'd been able to speak with someone wiser, I might have become aware sooner of how unhealthy my relationship was. Be careful any time the only voice of advisement is your own. Your judgment is easily clouded when you're in love.

2. *Being prepared.* When my children are old enough, I will tell them this story. I know it doesn't paint either of their parents in the best light, but I want them to learn from it. If I had been less naïve and known more about self-respect, I think I would have seen our relationship for what it was.

3. *Someone else's shoes.* If you told the story of your relationship—both the good and the bad—would there be more good or more bad? If a friend or a stranger heard about my relationship, and if I walked them through all of the stuff that was hurting me, I can't imagine them not wanting to shake me until my teeth rattled. Imagine someone else describing your relationship to you. Would they say your relationship is healthy? If the answer is no, or if you even have to question it, I beg you to take a deeper look at the relationship in your life.

CHAPTER 6

The Lie:

NO IS THE FINAL ANSWER

When asked to be a keynote speaker at a conference, I usually get to choose to some extent what I will talk about. Sometimes it's about business, life, or a more niche area of expertise, such as event planning. But the one thing most of my speeches have in common—the one thing I truly believe myself to be an expert on—is being told no. Truly, I've been told no in so many different ways and by so many different people that sometimes it seems as if *life* itself is saying no. I am an expert in rejection—or more specifically, I am an expert in bouncing back from rejection and fighting my way toward my goal.

I suppose if I can gift you anything in the reading of this book, it's that no is only an answer if you accept it. So allow me to use one chapter of this book to—I hope—light a fire under your butt. I want you to be so pumped up you can hardly stand it. I want you to have one of those nights when you stay up until one a.m. writing long lists of big dreams and plans. You know those nights—when you're so excited you can't shut off your brain and you end up having to take a Benadryl just to fall asleep?

Yes!

I want these words to excite you *that* much. I'm hoping some of my excitement rubs off on you—which, granted, would be way easier if I were giving you this speech in person—but I promise to use lots of italicized words for *emphasis* and to tell you about the word *no* and the role it's played in my life.

I waited years for the opportunity to explain my relationship with rejection . . . a lifetime, maybe.

About six years ago *Inc. Magazine* named me as one of their top thirty entrepreneurs under the age of thirty. Ooh la la!

It was a huge honor (I mean, clearly, because I'm still talking about it), but the really interesting thing that most people don't know is that when you get a prestigious title like that, almost immediately you begin to make hundreds of millions of dollars a year.

Just kidding!

No, what happens is, every college within a hundred-mile radius immediately starts calling and asking if you'll come and talk to their students. Since I haven't stopped speaking since the moment I figured out how, of course I accepted every single request. Each of those sessions lasted about an hour, which consisted of thirty minutes of me chatting about my career and my company and thirty minutes of questions and answers. After a while, I could almost time to the minute when I would hear the classic question: "Hi, Rachel," they'd always begin (because apparently we call adults by their first names now like we're a bunch of hippies!). "Can you tell us the secret of your success? Like, what's the one thing that truly gives you an advantage over others?"

First of all, God bless our youth. God bless these wee infants who believe that a lifetime of hustling and working and sweating and stressing and building, building, building a company could be summarized with one single answer.

But I tried.

At first when I was asked this question, I would give generic answers: hard work, dedication, making yourself indispensable, blah, blah, blah. But the more I went to schools and realized it was going to be the one question I got asked every time, I decided I'd better figure out the truth. So I began to ask myself questions.

What led to this massive platform and all of these fans? How did I get book deals and TV appearances? Why was *I* the one standing at the front of the classroom answering questions? Why not somebody else?

I think the obvious place to start is my family connections.

So, after graduating from Yale, and then later Harvard Business School, I began working in my family's oil business. I later went on to be a part owner of the Texas Rangers before becoming governor of that great state and then—I mean, most everyone knows that my father was a former president, so when I decided to run for president myself . . . Wait, no, that's not me.

That's George W. Bush!

No, as a reminder, I grew up in a place called Weedpatch. That wasn't a cute name for locals; that's literally its moniker on any map that wants to include it. The point is, family connections haven't been the secret to my success.

Seriously, though, after I moved to Los Angeles I started to gain some pretty influential friends within the entertainment industry. Paris Hilton and I became incredibly close. Later I went on to date Ray J (remember him?), and it really shot me into celebrity status. I used the attention from that relationship to get my own show on E! and then made millions with many kinds of products. When Kanye asked me to be his wife, well . . . Wait, shoot, nope. That's Kim Kardashian.

The secret to my success isn't celebrity status.

All joking aside, my success has a lot to do with waking up early, being the hardest-working person in the room, asking for help, being able to fail over and over again, and working constantly to improve both myself and my brand. But plenty of people do those things and don't experience the kind of success I have.

You want to know what it is? Why I believe I'm the one writing this book right now when people who've tried to do exactly the same things I have haven't succeeded?

It's simple, actually.

It's not about talent, skill, money, or connections.

It's because when they went after their dreams and came up against a roadblock, when they experienced rejection, or when someone or something told them no . . . they listened.

I am successful because I refused to take no for an answer. I am successful because I have never once believed my dreams were someone else's to manage. That's the incredible part about your dreams: nobody gets to tell you how big they can be.

When it comes to your dreams, no is not an answer. The word *no* is not a reason to stop. Instead, think of it as a detour or a yield sign. No means *merge with caution*. No reminds you to slow down—to re-evaluate where you are and to judge how the new position you're in can better prepare you for your destination.

In other words, if you can't get through the front door, try the side window. If the window is locked, maybe you slide down the chimney. No doesn't mean that you stop; it simply means that you change course in order to make it to your destination.

I realize, though, that not everybody looks at no the way I do. In order to inspire you to run headlong after your dreams, I may have to shift your perception of no. I'm going to give you everything I can think of to get you there . . . and I'm going to start with this question:

What if life isn't happening *to you*?

What if the hard stuff, the amazing stuff, the love, the joy, the hope, the fear, the weird stuff, the funny stuff, the stuff that takes you so low you're lying on the floor crying and thinking, *How did I get here?* . . .

What if none of it is happening *to you*?

What if all of it is happening *for* you?

It's all about perception, you guys.

Perception means we don't see things as *they are*; we see things as *we are*. Take a burning house. To a fireman, a burning house is a job to do—maybe even his life's work or mission. For an arsonist? A burning house is something exciting and good. What if it's your house? What if it's your family who's standing outside watching every earthly possession you own burning up? That burning house becomes something else entirely.

You don't see things as they are; you see things through the lens of what you think and feel and believe. Perception is reality, and I'm here to tell you that your reality is colored much more by your past experiences than by what is actually happening to you. If your past tells you that nothing ever works out, that life is against you, and that you'll never succeed, then how likely are you to keep fighting for something you want? Or, on the flip side, if you quit accepting no as the end of the conversation whenever you run up against opposition, you can shift your perception and fundamentally reshape your entire life.

Every single part of your life—your gratitude, the way you manage stress, how kind you are to others, how happy you are—can be changed by a shift in your perception. I don't have an entire book to devote to this topic, so today I'm just going to focus on your dreams. Let's talk about the goals you have for your life and how you can help yourself achieve them.

In order to do that, you have to name your goals. You have to shout out your hopes and dreams like the Great Bambino calling his shot. You need the courage to stand up and say, "This one, right here: this is mine!"

Before you continue reading, take a few moments to focus on a specific dream. Get out a piece of paper and write it down. Maybe write down ten dreams . . . maybe start with little innocuous things and keep writing until the truth comes out. Come on, girl—no one is watching. There's nobody here to judge.

Cue: elevator music.

All right. Do you have your dream?

Great! Maybe for some of you, that's the first time you've admitted that dream to yourself. But I'm willing to bet that most of you have met that dream before, even if you've never had the courage to put it down on paper.

Hello, old friend.

Perhaps it's been around since childhood . . . maybe it's something you're currently working on . . . maybe you used to work on it but gave up. Either way, if this is still a dream you have, then chances are, you've experienced some rejection where this dream is concerned. So my first mission is to change the way you see the word *no*—to take away your fear of it. Fear is driving your choices and affecting your decisions, so let's take the fear away. The best way I know to do that is to talk about it.

The Bible says, let that which is in the darkness be brought into the light. When things are allowed to sit in the darkness, when we're afraid to speak them aloud, we give them power. The darkness lets those fears fester and grow until they become stronger over time. If you never allow your fears out, then how in the world can you disseminate them?

Why do you think every chapter of this book begins with a lie I used to believe? Because I want to encourage you to speak your own lies into the world. The trouble is, we rarely know they are lies until someone points them out or we get past them. Before we can name them, they just disguise themselves as things we're afraid of. Think about it.

So let's take the fear away. Let's go through some of the reasons why people give up on their dreams. I want you to ask yourself if any of these examples sound like you.

Some people quit because a voice of authority tells them to. *Voice of authority* can mean all sorts of things . . . Maybe your first boss said you weren't right for your dream job, and you believed it. Maybe a parent—out of love or fear or caution or their own issues—told you not to try. Maybe a spouse or partner or best friend was afraid of what would happen to your relationship if you grew and so they tried to keep you anchored to the ground. Maybe that voice of authority said you're not "right" for it. Someone said you're too fat to train for a marathon or that you're too young to build your own business. They said you're too old to take dance lessons. They said you're too female to travel by yourself.

Maybe the voice of authority is your own. Maybe the negative self-talk in your head has been playing on repeat for your entire life.

Maybe an entire industry of experts is saying you're not right.

I have wanted to be an author for as long as I've understood that books were created by actual people. Like most wannabe authors, I started approximately seventy-three manuscripts but never actually finished a single one. Then, several years ago, I decided to stop giving up . . . *Just once*, I thought. *Just once I'd like to know what it's like to finish!*

So I began working on my historical-fiction-meets-time-travel book (because, I mean, *why not* write that on weekends?). Out of the blue I was approached by a literary agent. (Okay, just to give context, I suppose it wasn't out of the blue. I was a popular blogger and had built up a following of fans as well as a lot of publicity as a celebrity party planner by this time.)

The lit agent asked me if I'd ever considered writing a book. Of course I started regaling her with tales of my time-traveling historical romance—which, in case you're wondering, is basically every literary agent's worst nightmare as a pitch from an unknown, unproven author. So this woman, bless her, read the first twenty pages of that Dumpster fire and politely came back a week later to inform me that it wasn't really her style. She'd actually been reaching out to see if I wanted to do a nonfiction book on party planning. Since I was expressing an interest in fiction, though, she wondered if I'd be interested in writing a roman à clef. I'd never even heard of that term, but a quick Google search informed me that it's fiction about actual notable people. You just change the names to keep yourself from getting sued. A great example is *The Devil Wears Prada*. The agent's question was whether or not I had any juicy stories after having survived years of celebrity events.

Boy, did I ever!

As soon as we got off the phone, I knew the story immediately.

I knew the story because it was *my* story. I'd moved from a small Southern-minded town to Los Angeles as a teenager. Before I was old enough to drink legally, I was working parties for the biggest A-list celebrities on the planet. I was a fish out of water and always awkward, but somehow built a career within that space. I didn't even have to dream up material; I had years of stories so juicy I couldn't have made them up if I tried.

I wrote ten pages and emailed them to her right away.

Two days later she wrote back: *I can sell this all day long!*

A literary agent . . . a real-life, legit literary agent told me that she could sell my book if I was willing to finish it. I nearly choked on my joy.

I became obsessed. I barely saw my husband or my kids as I wrote like an insane person until my first draft was finished. I kept telling myself that the only reason I didn't have a book deal already was because I'd never actually finished a manuscript . . . so I believed this book was fated. I imagined in intricate detail what it would be like to hold the published copy in my hands.

I did finish the book, and the literary agent sent it to every publisher in New York. The initial responses were so kind and encouraging. Editors would write long emails back explaining why it wasn't for them but telling me how much they'd enjoyed it. My belief that we were going to sell it only increased when three other publishers asked for conference calls to discuss it.

When I dialed into the first call, I thought I was going to pee my pants.

When we got on the phone, the publishing team started by telling me how much they liked me, my online presence, my writing style, etc. They praised the book as funny and cute . . . good things, as far as I knew.

"Our concern," said the editor, "is that it's too sweet."

I had no idea what that meant, but since it was my first book, I assured them that anything like that could be fixed in an edit.

"We were hoping you'd be open to changes."

"Of course!" I assured them. I'd be open to ritual sacrifice if it meant selling my first book.

"So you'd feel comfortable adding some steam?"

Y'all, I had no idea what she was talking about. My brain conjured up the image of a manhole cover with steam coming out.

"What exactly did you have in mind?" I hedged.

"Sex. It needs sex, Rachel. No young woman in her early twenties who lives in LA is a virgin. Nobody will believe this love story. If you spice it up, this could be a bestseller."

I'm trying to remember if I've ever been so uncomfortable in a professional setting in my life.

For context, it's important to note that this was right when *Fifty Shades of Grey* was breaking into the book world. Since publishing chases trends like any other industry, every editor was hyperfocused on trying to tap into that fan base.

I had zero idea how to respond to them. Y'all, I'm no saint. I've read books with sex in them before (don't tell my Mema!), but I had no earthly clue that someone would ever ask me to write it. Also, I loved that the heroine of my book was naïve and innocent—and I thought that's what made her special. The more they tried to convince me to write steam into my book, the more I wondered if I was in an after-school special. Like, *Hey, Rachel, just smoke this crack and we'll be friends with you.*

I politely declined.

"We totally understand," they told me. "But without that element, this book is too sweet for the market. Nobody will buy it as is."

I was devastated.

Two more calls with publishers went exactly the same way.

Then one after another, every publisher left on our submission list turned it down. It was a Friday afternoon when the very last publisher passed. I remember locking myself in the bathroom and sobbing. And, you guys, these were not gentle, beautiful tears. This was like, *my dreams are over / everyone hates my book / I am a terrible writer* UGLY tears.

I can't tell you how long I stayed down on the bathroom tile, but I can tell you that I eventually got back up. I dried my tears and walked to the kitchen to pour a glass of wine. Then I sat down at my crappy laptop where I'd written my terrible prudish manuscript that nobody wanted and Googled, *How do you self-publish a book?*

In February 2014, I self-published *Party Girl* about a naïve, sweet, and, yes, virginal party planner in her early twenties living in LA.

That first weekend I think it sold fifty copies—and likely forty-five of those were bought by Dave. Every week, though, I'd sell a few here and a handful there. The sales kept growing, and people were passing it around to their friends. As it turns out, the sweetness of the main character was the exact thing that people liked about the book. Six months later a publisher called and asked if they could buy it from me and offered me a deal for two more books to turn it into a series.

To date, that single book, the one I was told no one would buy, has sold over a hundred thousand copies. It also launched my career as an author.

Here's the most important piece of that whole story. Are you paying attention?

If I had listened to the experts, that book would still be sitting on my computer today.

Nobody—not a voice of authority, not your mama, not the foremost expert in your arena—gets to tell you how big your dreams can be. They can talk all they want . . . but you get to decide if you're willing to listen.

Another reason people give up on their dreams? It's difficult and/or it's taking too long.

Goals and dreams are hard. I get it. Actually accomplishing them is *so* much harder than you think it will be. Maybe you're making progress, but it's only an inch at a time—meanwhile, your friend Tammy has been promoted twice, your sister is married with two kids, and you feel as though you're still way back there at the start when everyone is passing you by. Some days you feel so discouraged you want to cry.

Go ahead and cry.

Rend your garments and wail to the heavens like some biblical mourner. Get it all out. Then dry your eyes and wash your face and keep on going. You think this is hard? That's because *it is*. So what? Nobody said it would be easy.

You're tired? How many times in your life have you been tired but you found a way to keep going? How many of you reading this right now have given up on a dream because it was exhausting to keep chasing it? In that same vein, how many of you have ever gone through labor? Even if you haven't before, I know you can understand the gist. No matter how you bring a baby into the world (even through adoption), it's emotionally and physically exhausting—but somehow you find a way through. You dig down deep for strength you didn't know you had because the process is literally life or death.

Don't tell me you don't have it in you to want something more for your life. Don't tell me you have to give up because it's difficult. This is life or death too. This is the difference between living a life you always dreamed of or sitting alongside the death of the person you were meant to become. That's what it feels like to me when I've given up on a dream, even for a little while—as if I'm at a wake. As if I'm sitting in a room and looking at the evidence of what could have been. I'm sure many of you know what that's like, and you either want to change it or keep yourself from getting there in the first place.

You have to do something about it. You have to reach down inside yourself and remember the reason you started this. You'd better find the will to keep going, because if you don't, I promise you *someone else will*. If that happens, girl, you will watch someone else achieve *your* dreams and enjoy the spoils of their hard-fought battle. And if that happens, you will understand one of the greatest lessons in this life: the only thing worse than giving up is wishing that you hadn't.

You think your dream is taking too long? It took Julia Child ten years to write *Mastering the Art of French Cooking*. Her work changed cooking for people all over the world and launched her career. James Cameron worked on *Avatar* for fifteen years, and it is the most successful film in the history of time.

On January 3, 1870, ground was broken for the construction of the Brooklyn Bridge. The project took ten years, and during that time, the lives of so many men on the building crew were lost. But, you guys, the Brooklyn Bridge still stands as a symbol of New York, and 135 years later, it brings forty-three million cars to and from Manhattan every single year.

Don't you get it? Nothing that lasts is accomplished quickly. Nobody's entire legacy is based on a single moment, but rather the collection of one's experiences. If you're lucky, your legacy will be a lifetime in the making.

Between my event company and the media business I run

now, it's taken me thirteen years of work to get to this place—and not one of those years was wasted. I needed thirteen years to gain the knowledge to write to you about this topic. I needed thirteen years of speaking to college students, MOPS groups, and panel discussions to build my skill enough to give the keynote speech that served as the inspiration for this chapter. I needed to fail at public speaking and make mistakes over and over again to learn how to do that. I needed to write crappy manuscripts that I never finished and then one that nobody wanted to buy. I needed to fight my way into the publishing industry and spend years making my presence known before I was in a place where someone would give me the opportunity for a book like this.

I needed to endure personal hardships and discouragement and one rejection on top of another—all so I could stand right here and say to you, "Your dream is worth fighting for, and while you're not in control of what life throws at you, you are in control of the fight."

The last reason people give up on their dreams?

Something traumatic gets in your way. Disaster is the ultimate excuse. Divorce or illness or something far worse happens to you, and sometimes the goals slip quietly into the background and get left there. We leave them because this trauma is so heavy we just can't carry one more thing. Sometimes trauma happens, and if we're being honest, a part of us rejoices, thinking, *Well, now nobody can expect anything else from me because it's miracle enough that I'm upright.*

Let me take a moment to tell those of you who are dealing with and fighting through something painful: it is a miracle that you're sitting here. You are nobly doing your best to battle your way through it. You are a warrior because of the trials you are going through, but don't you dare squander the strength you have earned just because the acquisition of it was painful.

Those are the most important stories to share.

You can use that strength to pave a path for others to follow along behind. I've shared many of my own painful stories in the chapters of this book, and none of them have been easy to talk about; but I do it because I hope that by sharing them I'm able to help some of you who've walked through similar things. I've also talked about my own goals and dreams and the ways I've pushed myself to achieve them. Every single one of those dreams has served a purpose in my life. Sometimes it was a small change and sometimes it was life-changing, but in every circumstance, I grew for having walked through it. Friends, it's not about the goal or the dream you have. It's about who you *become* on your way to that goal.

When a voice of authority says it's taking too long, you're too "fat, old, tired, or female" for it, or your trauma is too big . . . do you know what they are giving you?

Permission to quit.

You're already scared, you're already second-guessing your-self, and when someone or something comes along and speaks into that *exact thing* you were already questioning, you think, *Yep, that's what I thought. I give up.*

Look again at those dreams you wrote down on your paper at the start of this chapter. Now listen to me:

You do not have permission to quit!

I revoke that permission! I take away the power those people or circumstances put over your life, and I give it back to you.

You think it's not that easy? Of course it is. This is all about perception, right? Your perception of what's holding you back is currently big and bad and terrifying, but those obstacles are only real if you believe in them.

It's all in your hands now. Everything that happens from here on out is entirely up to you. This is the hard part because I will tell you right now: nobody will ever care about your dream as much as you do. Ever.

Do you hear me, sister?

Whether you want to lose weight or write a book or be on TV or travel the world on a speaking tour, you are the steward of your own dreams! Maybe you want to own your own home, get your degree, or save your marriage. Maybe it's a shop on Etsy, opening a small business, or getting the lead in the local production of *Oklahoma!* this fall. Whatever it is, big or small, grandiose or simple, *nobody* can care about it the way you do!

Even if you have a supportive family. Even if you have the greatest friends alive. Even if your spouse is the most uplifting, encouraging human and your number one fan . . . even then, girl, they will not want it as much as you do.

It doesn't keep them up at night. It doesn't light their soul on fire.

It's your dream.

Your own special wish that your heart made long before you were even conscious of it. You want to see it come to fruition? Well then, you have to understand that nobody can take it away from you and ultimately nobody is going to help you achieve it. Not really.

You have to decide to pursue your wildest dreams. No matter what they are, no matter how simple or extravagant. No matter if they seem ridiculous to others or maybe even too easy . . . it doesn't matter. They're your dreams, and you are allowed to chase them— not because you are more special or talented or well-connected, but because you are worthy of wanting something more.

Because you are worthy of not letting your past dictate your future.

Start today. Start right now, this very second, and promise yourself—heck, promise *me*—that you'll reach for the big stuff.

Do you want the big stuff for your life?

You won't get there by saying yes. Yes is the easy part. You'll get there by not giving up when you hear the word *no*.

THINGS THAT HELPED ME . . .

1. **Audacity.** It's pretty audacious to ignore what other people, even experts, are telling you is right. I think we could all use a little more audacity around these parts. I don't mean that you need to become militant or disrespectful; I just mean you should keep your eyes on your goal, regardless of what gets in your way.

2. **Alternate paths.** I worry when I give this advice that some random person who listens to the idea of not giving up on her dreams will hear, "Go harass people until they give you what you want." That's not going to get anybody anywhere, and we all know it. Use the no you hear as an indication that you should try an alternative route.

3. **Keeping my goals in plain sight.** It's easy to focus on your goals when you're fired up or excited about a new project, but focusing becomes harder when life interferes with your direct access to keep working on it. So pin up your dream somewhere you can see it. I'm a big fan of displaying visuals inside my closet door to remind me every single day of what my aim is. Currently taped to my door: the cover of *Forbes* featuring self-made female CEOs, a vacation house in Hawaii . . . and a picture of Beyoncé, obvi.

CHAPTER 7

The lie:

I'M BAD AT SEX

I used to be really bad at sex.

Whoa, Nelly!

You didn't think I was going there—but I totally am. I'm going to talk about sex as a married, Christian woman, and I hope it'll be okay.

My husband? He's likely hiding under a rock right now because me writing about this is definitely his worst nightmare.

My worst nightmare is getting chased by Bigfoot, so I guess we all have our crosses to bear, Dave.

But Dave shouldn't be worried. I'm not writing about him; I'm writing about me . . . and my bad sex. I'm choosing to write about this big, scary, embarrassing thing at the risk of petrifying my in-laws and giving Mema a heart attack because I think it's important. I don't think women talk about it enough.

Oh sure, the *world* talks about it. As much as it can, as loud as it can, as often as it can . . . but not in a realistic way. Not in a way that makes tangible sense to a virginal clarinet player whose experience with men when she met her husband was equal to her experience with hunting large game in the African wilds. Which is to say none. None at all.

My early opportunities for sexual education included ladies at church (who didn't speak about it within my hearing) or media as a whole, which showed me an ideal that was impossible to achieve. So I walked into my marriage with *no realistic idea* of what to expect. Which is flipping ridiculous! I wish just *one time* before I got married someone had said, "Look, here are my experiences. Here's what you need to know, here's what you should consider, and also, the first few times you have sex you should pee afterward so you don't get a UTI!"

Somewhere in Texas an older reader just fainted.

Yes, I wrote about a urinary tract infection. If that freaks you out, move right along to the next chapter, sister, because it's going to get way more intimate than that.

I knew very little about sex other than what I had gleaned from TV or movies . . . so I was terrible at it. And not terrible as in awkward (though I was most definitely that). It was terrible because I was miserable, and I made my husband miserable too. Five years into our marriage, our sex life was nearly nonexistent. By comparison, we'll celebrate our fourteenth wedding anniversary this year—and now our sex life is the stuff of legends!

No, seriously. We do it more than any married couple you know—or at least more often than most married couples with four kids and two full-time jobs. We have sex not out of obligation but because it's really, really good. When it's really good, why would you not go at it like a couple of howler monkeys whenever you can?

Today, it's awesome. But it was a *long* road from there to here, and I'm going to tell you all about it in case you find yourself in the same place . . . and because I don't want you to get a UTI. Listen up.

I met Dave when I was nineteen years old and he was twenty-seven. I had never even been on a date before, and he didn't know how much younger I was than him. As I've already told you, when the truth came out a couple of months in, it went over like an obese cat falling off the back fence. It was an ungraceful and violent fall, but we still landed on our feet.

Dave has been my best friend since that first year together. He is my favorite human on the planet, and I love him so much it makes my heart want to explode. When we got married, we had the happiest life I could've possibly dreamed up for myself. And as for sex? We did it like rabbits. We did it like rabbits because that's what you're supposed to do as newlyweds, right?

How many times could we do it in a day?

How many times in an hour?

I would do it in the rain, in the dark, on a train, in a car, in a tree . . .

You get the point, Sam I Am. We were having a lot of sex.

And I loved it.

I loved it because being physically close with him made me feel cherished and adored. I loved it because it made him so happy. It made us so happy. We were newlyweds, we were having sex, and life was good.

But as the first couple of years went on and the newness wore off, the joy of the honeymoon phase wore off too. In the beginning my excitement made me bold. As time went on, though, I felt less comfortable, as if a switch had been flipped. I was raised to be this good Christian girl. Now I was supposed to be a sex kitten, but I had no idea how.

So I drank.

We'd go on a date and I'd have just enough wine to feel sexy. Then I'd try and do sexy things or act in a sexy way, but I rarely enjoyed it as much as he did. Did I pretend to enjoy it? Heck yes! That's what you're supposed to do, right? Then I started to resent the fact that I wasn't enjoying it, resented that I thought I should have sex even when I wasn't that excited about it.

Then I had a baby, and my body morphed and my stomach stretched out and my boobs leaked and I was exhausted. Sex was basically the least enjoyable thing I could imagine. But I kept doing it, kept pretending that I loved every second. I never once talked to Dave about how I was feeling—I was too embarrassed and unsure. I was also nervous about hurting his feelings, so I kept it to myself. More time passed, and our sex life was hanging by a thread. By the time our second son was a toddler, sex barely happened at all—and when I came out of the fog of being a mother of two and thought enough to ask Dave about it, the answer was hard to hear.

"Why don't we have sex anymore?" I asked him one night.

He looked at me as though the question hurt his feelings.

"I got tired of being shot down."

I was immediately defensive. "I don't shoot you down. I always say yes."

"You might agree, Rachel, but you don't actually want to, and that's worse than not having it at all."

Initially, I was pretty annoyed. Here I was taking one for the team, and he was hurt because I wasn't more enthusiastic. But the more I thought about it, the more I understood how right he was. I might've been agreeing to sex, but I was stiff and uncomfortable, tired and unenthusiastic. Agreeing to it did not mean I was embracing it. My husband could tell I wasn't enjoying it, so rather than asking me to participate halfway, he had just stopped asking altogether. What a bummer.

They say the first step to fixing something is admitting you have a problem.

Now, I know many of you are super in touch with your own feminine mystique. You've got the whole sex thing down pat, and you have a hundred orgasms a week. Good for you, sister. Seriously, you're my hero! And the following advice probably isn't for you. For you, what I have to say will sound trite and basic or maybe even naïve. That's cool, because these are the things that worked for me, and I share them in case they are helpful to someone who is like me (or who I used to be).

Here are the steps I took to go from being bad at sex to being exceptional at sex. There are seven of them . . . one for every day of the week.

THINGS THAT HELPED ME . . .

1. *I redefined sex in my own mind.* For the longest time, sex symbolized a lot of things—and not all of them were positive. I decided to change what I thought sex was . . . This might not be what sex is for you, your friends, or the Holy Ghost and all the saints; but going forward I decided that sex was supposed to be a fun experience that would *always* be more compelling than whatever else I could be doing. Up until that point I was continuously weighing sex against other things (reading a book, watching TV, etc.)—and it was playing second fiddle. But if I reminded myself that sex was always an awesome opportunity, then I would presumably want to choose it.

2. *I figured out how sex could be an earth-shattering experience.* When you're uncomfortable or don't feel sexy or are nervous or shy or whatever, you're not going to enjoy yourself. If you're not enjoying yourself, you're not having good sex. So I asked myself: How can I enjoy this more? What's holding me back? The answer? Me. Next I spoke with Dave about all the things I was thinking and feeling. It shocked me that after all our years together I could still be so embarrassed, but I pushed through it. We needed to be on the same page, and the only way to get there was by opening up the book and talking to him about it.

3. *I read Hebrews 13:4.* Part of my hang-ups were related to my being a good Christian girl who couldn't reconcile becoming a freak in the sheets. And then I read Hebrews 13:4: "Let marriage be held in honor among all, and let the bed be undefiled" (WEB). Now, straight up, I'm sure I'm not reading this right. I'm sure someone who studied theology will tell me that this actually means something different. But what I read, or what I take away when I read that line, is that the things that happen in my bed with my husband cannot be weird or bad or wrong. Let me back up and say there are definitely things that a committed, monogamous couple can do sexually that can be incredibly hurtful to them both. Pornography, for example, is extremely damaging to both the consumer and the people being used as objects for your lust. But the other stuff? Lingerie, leather, toys, role-play, trying every position possible, going at it on the kitchen table, dirty talk, *whatever* . . . If it turns you on and doesn't hurt you, I say go for it!

4. *I embraced my body.* Having a low opinion of your body is so damaging to your ability to enjoy sex. I used to worry about whether or not my tummy was tight or if my butt looked okay

in those panties. You know what Dave was thinking when I took off my clothes? *Boobies!* Your partner is just thrilled you showed up, and all those things you're questioning aren't helping anyone. I practiced positive self-talk about how great my butt looked or how sexy I was. I did it so much that at some point, I started to believe it.

5. *I committed to my orgasm.* Okay, just writing that line makes me blush. I'm imagining some future book-signing where a reader comes up to my table and says, "So . . . you committed to your orgasm." But this is important, and even if it embarrasses me I want you to know it. Back in the day, when we first started having sex, an orgasm for me was like icing on the cake. But here's the thing, ladies: *Orgasms are not icing on the cake.* Orgasms *are* the cake! A *second orgasm* is icing on the cake! Remember how I said that I had to figure out how to make sex the greatest thing ever? Remember how I told you that I wanted to desire it over anything else in my life? You know how you do that? With orgasms! I decided years ago that I would never, *and I mean never*, again have sex that didn't include an orgasm for me. When I told Dave this plan, he agreed it was the greatest idea I'd ever come up with. Because here's the thing: for most of us, our partners are thrilled to give us pleasure; and if we're both committed to my orgasm at the outset, it will happen.

6. *I had to figure out what turns me on.* Oh sure, I'd been turned on many times in my life, but I'd never truly considered the difference between what really did it for me and what was just situational. Knowing what turns me on was key because, remember, my orgasms were our new endgame, and I don't know how to have one without being turned on. So we

experimented until I learned myself and my body better. (Feel free to head back up to the *undefiled marriage bed* paragraph for a list of ideas.)

7. *We committed to having sex every day for a month.* Years ago, at the outset of changing up our sex lives, Dave and I initiated something we called Sexy September. We vowed to have sex every day during the month of September—*no excuses.* It was pretty daunting in the beginning, especially with full-time jobs and two little kids. But the end result was fantastic! It gave me the opportunity to experiment and try things out without any pressure. Also, shockingly, having more sex made us want to . . . have more sex. I highly encourage you to pick your own sexy month and go for it!

CHAPTER 8

The Lie:

I DON'T KNOW HOW
TO BE A MOM

I'm the worst pregnant woman you've ever met in your life. No, really. I hate basically every part of pregnancy except the baby you get at the end.

I have friends who love it. Like, capital *L-O-V-E*, wish they could carry one hundred babies and be pregnant forever. I fully support their earth mother calling and the obvious joy they find in being a vessel for human life.

But I don't share it.

I am thankful for my pregnancies—so stinking thankful to the bottom of my heart that God blessed me with the ability to carry three beautiful little boys to term. I do not take this for granted when I know so many women who pray for the same blessing have not received it.

But every single part of pregnancy is hard on me.

The morning sickness never *once* went away after the morning, nor did it end after the first trimester. I put on pregnancy weight like it was my part-time job, then felt incapable of taking it off. My back hurt, my feet hurt, and during my first pregnancy, I got a varicose vein in the *most terrible place* a human being can get a varicose vein—which meant I had to wear special "weight bearing" underwear with each consecutive pregnancy. Sidenote: If you ever are curious about the easiest way to crush a gal's spirit, I'd recommend searching "groin support panties" on the internet.

But I digress.

The point is, I'm pretty bad at pregnancy. On top of everything else I've mentioned, I also dealt with unrelenting fear.

What if I ate bologna and contracted listeria?

What if my blueberry-sized fetus developed some rare disease since the last time I'd had an ultrasound?

What if all the Carl's Jr. chicken strips I was eating gave him high cholesterol?

What if the cord wrapped around his neck?

What if the room wasn't ventilated enough when I painted the nursery?

What if the placenta previa didn't clear up?

What if that vodka Red Bull I drank when I was two weeks pregnant (but didn't yet know it) had hurt him?

Seriously, though. What if the cord wrapped around his neck??

The worries were overbearing, and I managed them with the dignity of a geriatric terrier—which is to say, I barked at anyone who got too close, and I needed a special stepstool to hoist myself in and out of bed.

When the blessed event finally occurred, I was ecstatic. First, because I was finally going to meet Jackson Cage—a child we had dreamed up and named on a cross-country road trip years before. Also, I was finally going to have my body back to myself. I was euphoric to have made it through the labor, something I honestly believed would be the toughest part of motherhood.

But at home with Jackson in all his perfect glory, I was unprepared for how inadequate I'd feel as a new mom. I loved him obsessively. I was also terrified of him. All the fears I had while he was inside of me suddenly multiplied by a hundred million. I barely slept at night because I was positive he'd stop breathing if I wasn't there to watch him do it. Breastfeeding was hard and painful, and I never produced enough milk to feed the giant offspring Dave and I created. We had to supplement with formula, we had to learn how to manage his reflux, we had to navigate a middle-of-the-night ER visit when he got a high fever at seven weeks old—all while dealing with the soul-sucking loss of sleep. My husband has always been my best friend and my favorite human on earth, but I remember once, when Jackson was about a month and a half old, looking at Dave and sincerely believing I *hated* him. Like, to the pit of my soul *hated* him.

I like to tell young married couples about the time I hated Dave. I like to tell them because I want them to know how this feeling is totally normal and they'll likely find themselves there now and again. Jackson was six weeks old—which, by the way, friends, is the most probable week for real unadulterated hatred—and he was still waking up in the night.

It's important to emphasize the word *still* here because I think my young, ignorant, pre-child self thought we'd be back to neutral and coasting toward parental bliss by the end of month one.

Bless my precious, childlike heart.

Becoming new parents is such a fake-out. The first two weeks you're deep in euphoria and, yes, it's hard, but people are bringing you casseroles and your mama is still in town to help and you have this perfect little cherub whom you love so much you want to bite the chubby cheeks right off his face. And then the next couple of weeks go by and you settle into a zombie routine. Your boobs start to leak through your clothes, and you haven't bathed in a week. Also, your hair is literally the most terrible it's ever been, but whatever. *You're getting through it.*

But by six weeks, the wheels start to fall off.

You're thinking, *Why am I so exhausted?*

Why do I still look like I'm five months pregnant?

Why am I still spending all my time nursing?

And what punk invented cluster feeding? Because I will punch him right in his stupid face!

At six weeks, I was a little, um, *frustrated* with how much I was doing to care for our baby. In other words, I didn't feel Dave was being that helpful and the responsibility of managing most of it by myself was overwhelming. I didn't mention any of this to him, though. I just bottled it up nice and tight and shoved it down deep where it could never bother anybody. Everyone knows that's the best way to handle your problems, right? Then one day we were chatting about something, and Chernobyl fell out of his mouth.

"I'm tired."

That's what he said.

Those were the words.

My world shifted on its axis and my eyes widened to eight times their natural size, but he didn't notice. He was too busy talking: "I am just so exhausted from waking up early this morning, blah, blah, blah, more ill-conceived words."

You know that TV show *Snapped*?

It's a docu-style series about real-life crimes where women just snap and try to take down someone on the way.

That was me.

I went full-on Sybil. I was crying, I was laughing, I was trying to figure out who would raise this baby if I strangled Dave with the plastic tubing from my breast pump. To quote one of the most famous sayings in our entire marriage, I shouted/cried, "On my wedding day I never thought I could hate you as much as I hate you right now!"

It was not my best moment. But luckily for me, Dave, and all the other humans on this planet, relationships are full of opportunities for grace.

Even when the baby started sleeping (and *we* started sleeping), I was a mess. I loved Jackson, but I didn't really feel bonded to him. I was so terrified of doing something wrong that I never let myself relax. I was so focused on housework and chores and making sure his onesie stayed spotless that I never just enjoyed my time as a new mom. I think because I was so worried about failing him, I ended up failing myself.

Because I was so concerned with how we should all *look* as a family, I didn't take the time to let myself feel connected. I continued this pattern with my second son, Sawyer, so that when I became a mother of two, I had a serious case of postpartum depression. I spent almost every day imagining what it would be like to run away from home. I sat in our living room, breastfeeding my week-old baby while a twenty-month-old ran around a living room littered with toys and dirty diapers I hadn't yet thrown away, and I'd think, *I should just drive away and never look back. Everyone here would be better off without me.*

Because I didn't feel I was succeeding at being a mom—the *one thing* I should innately know how to do—I was positive I was a failure. In retrospect I can recognize that my perception of this role was based on images I saw online and in magazines, but at the time I was too sleep-deprived to know I was chasing an impossibility. I had spent so much time worrying about not living up to some Pinterest-worthy standard that I completely lost who I actually was. Oh, those were dark days. When I look at pictures of that time, my hair might be combed and I might even be wearing some lipstick—but my eyes look haunted.

So this chapter is for the new mamas or soon-to-be mamas. Listen up! You don't have to have it all figured out. You don't have to know everything. The mechanics of keeping a newborn alive are fairly simple. Feed it, cuddle it, love it, change it when it's wet, keep it warm, cuddle it again.

A new mother's daily list of goals should boil down to

1. Take care of the baby.
2. Take care of yourself.

Boom.

The end.

Darn it, you didn't get to the laundry today? Look at your list again: Did you take care of the baby? Yes. Did you take care of yourself? Also yes. Oh, I think you're crushing this new-mom business then. I guess the laundry can wait.

What's that, you're sad because you haven't lost the baby weight? Check out your handy-dandy to-do list with exactly two items on it. Is the baby still alive? Awesome. How about you—are you still breathing in and out? Well then, it looks like you're the greatest mom ever. Keep on trucking!

Pinterest is awesome, and decorating your nursery in perfectly coordinating colors is half the fun of having a child. Looking at Instagram? Heck, I still look at all those pregnant Instagrammers for adorable bump-appropriate wardrobe tips, and I'm not even pregnant! It makes sense to look outside ourselves when we're unsure about something new, and we are rarely as uncertain as we are during new motherhood. But let me tell you this—because I didn't understand it until years later . . .

The God who made the moon and the stars and the mountains and the oceans, the Creator who did all of those things, believed that *you* and your baby were meant to be a pair. That doesn't mean you're going to be a perfect fit. That doesn't mean you won't make mistakes. It does mean that you need not fear failure because *you can't fail a job you were created to do.*

Somewhere some cynical reader is thinking about all the parents who *do* fail. There are plenty of mamas who make bad choices, who hurt themselves or their children. As a former foster parent, I know firsthand that there are babies suffering right now from abuse and neglect, and even if a divine plan brought them to their mamas, it might not be the best answer for them to stay there.

But I'm not speaking about those mamas. I'm talking to you. Don't be overwhelmed with anxiety that your baby should be on a sleep schedule, eating organic foods, or sitting up by now. I'm talking to the person who is reading all of the books and all of the articles and feels overwhelmed by what's right when there are so many possible wrongs. The very fact that you are so concerned, sweet friend, means you're engaged and focused and dedicated to doing what's best. That makes you the best kind of parent. The rest will take care of itself.

THINGS THAT HELPED ME . . .

1. *Finding a tribe.* Join a church group, go to mommy-and-me yoga, or look online for a club to join. Look for a group of women who understand what it means to be a new mom too.

There is so much power in solidarity. There is so much grace when you're talking with someone who also has baby puke on her shirt.

2. **Staying away from Pinterest.** For the love of all that is holy, nobody should be allowed on Pinterest after a big life event. Why? Because you feel like you're missing out, or that your life, nursery, or post-baby body should look like what you're finding on the internet. Pay attention to what is giving you anxiety or making you question yourself. If it's social media, then do your heart a favor and take a break from it. I promise it will still be there when you're getting more sleep and feeling less emotional.

3. **Getting out of the house.** Every. Single. Day. The best thing you can do for yourself, your sanity, and your baby is to leave the scene of the crime. Leave the place with the dishes in the sink and the overflowing Diaper Genie. Put your baby in a carrier or a stroller and go on a walk around the neighborhood. Put in some headphones and listen to Beyoncé or Adele or a podcast on business ethics. Do whatever you have to do to remind yourself that there is a life beyond your nest and that you are still part of it.

4. **Talking to someone about my feelings.** An effective way for us to overcome lies is to speak them aloud to a partner. Whether you choose your spouse, your friend, or a trusted family member, sharing with them that you're struggling can give you the support you need to see all of the falsities that are popping up in your life.

CHAPTER 9

The Lie:

I'M NOT A GOOD MOM

If we're going to talk about how much I struggled as a new mom, then we also have to talk about how much I have struggled as a mom in general. Navigating what it means to be a mother while dealing with a newborn baby is brutal . . . but what comes next?

That's an emotional mind-screw of epic proportions.

When my oldest was seven, he crushed my soul over Cheerios.

"You know what you need, Mommy?" he asked me one morning while I was pouring cereal into a bowl shaped like a bulldog's face.

When a child gives you an opener like that, the conversation could go in any direction imaginable. Maybe I needed a superhero cape or a new spatula or pink hair. His train of thought could go anywhere.

"What?" I wanted to know. "What do I need?"

"You need one of those necklaces with our initials on them. You know, the ones with the letters for each kid's name?"

At the time monogram charm necklaces were all the rage.

"Yes, I know those necklaces."

"You should get one of those. All the moms at my school have them," he told me between bites. "You need to get one too."

"Okay . . ." I was a bit confused. "Why do I need to get one?"

He smiled at me happily.

"So you can finally be like all the other moms."

Finally.

Like all the other moms.

A handful of words shouldn't crush you—shouldn't make you question yourself as a mother. But when you're already questioning yourself, and then someone—not just your son but anyone—brings up the exact thing you've been worried about, it doesn't really take much to push you over the edge.

I hadn't worried about what my jewelry—or lack thereof—said about me as a mom, but I was glaringly aware of how different I was from the other mothers at Jackson's school events. I just didn't know that he'd noticed as well.

I grappled with his statement for days . . . His suggestion to be *like all the other moms* meant that he recognized I wasn't like them already. It meant that he saw me as different—and when you're little, all you really want is to be just like everybody else.

What he noticed is that I'm not like the other moms because I work . . . a lot. I very rarely get to drop him off at school or pick him up. Because of that, I made a special effort to volunteer in his classroom every other week—but that wasn't right either, because even though I sat in the teeny tiny chair cutting papers and stuffing homework folders like the other volunteers, I wasn't in jeans or yoga pants. I was in high heels and a white blazer that I should have known better than to wear on the day they were making teepees out of brown modeling clay. (Another mom was sure to point that out to me.) I was wearing that outfit because directly following that session at school I was heading to a meeting. Like most working moms, my life is a constant juggling act.

Sometimes it looks like a perfectly orchestrated ballet where I'm able to flit back and forth between the kids' activities and work activities. Other times it looks like a triage unit where I'm doing everything I can to keep up with the need around me and yet still dropping the ball on priorities that feel like they are slipping away before I can get to them.

At the time I hoped that committing to extra projects for my boys would make up the difference. So I'd overwhelm an already overwrought schedule by agreeing to plan the big fund-raiser for their class, or being on the board at preschool, or taking off an afternoon to cover soccer practice. I thought the extra effort would win me brownie points with my boys, but it didn't. My children were little, and their memory stretched only as far as yesterday. Even now they don't care about today's business trip, my looming book deadline, or the staff at my office who count on me to pull my weight. My kids care that their friends' moms went on the museum field trip yesterday and I didn't because I was flying to Chicago for work.

Having kids in school feels stressful for me. My three little people have totally different schedules to keep track of, and my baby girl has her own agenda. There's paperwork: both the kind that accumulates in massive piles in the first couple of weeks and the loose-leaf permission slips and sign-up forms that I find shoved into backpacks throughout the year. Also, school lunches. I'm pretty regimented about using a system to keep their lunches organized, but now that the boys are older, they want to have lunch at school—but only on specific days. So now tracking the cafeteria calendar is a part-time job, as is making sure their lunch cards have enough money on them to get the teriyaki chicken this Thursday. There are field trips and performances. There are bake sales and carnivals. There are dropoffs and pickups and banking days when they get out an hour early, and if Jackson (God bless him!) didn't remind me about them, I'd likely forget every single one. There are so many things to remember, and I guess what ultimately stresses me out is the idea that other moms—at school or out there in the wild world—are somehow way better at keeping track of this than I am.

I am one of the most organized people I have ever met, and even with all of my planning, I still am constantly forgetting things—or remembering them at midnight the night before they're due. And no matter what I do or create or volunteer for, some mythical "other mom" at school has done it better.

"Yes, Mommy, you *can buy* the T-shirt we need for make-your-own-T-shirt day, but Liam's mom grew organic cotton plants. Then she hand-separated the seed from the fiber before spinning it into thread and fabric for the shirt she sewed him herself."

I can't even begin to keep up, and the stress of trying to do so can make me crazy.

So this year I made a big decision.

I'm over it. I am utterly over the idea of crushing back-to-school time—or any other part of school for that matter! I do some parts of it well. Our morning routine might be choreographed chaos, but we are never late to school. My kids (with the exception of the four-year-old) are well groomed and well mannered, and they get good grades. Beyond that, they are good people—the kind of kids who befriend the outcasts and the loners. Sure, they attack each other at home and are dramatic enough about their lack of access to technology to earn themselves Oscars, but whatever. We are doing pretty good—and pretty good is way better than trying to fake perfection any day of the week.

So I might not volunteer in the classroom this year—though count me in for store-bought goodies at the class parties. And I might not make it to every field trip, because even if it means I'm the jerk of all jerks, I hate chaperoning field trips. Also—gird your loins—a babysitter will likely pick up my boys from school more than I will. I wish our town would extend more grace for this . . . perhaps the same level of grace extended to working fathers who aren't able to make pickup either?

Mom, you should parent in whatever way works for your family and spend less time worrying about other people's perceptions of how you're doing. Can we stop being so hard on ourselves and instead focus on the good work we are doing, the results of which are evident in the awesome little people we're raising?

What if we all went into the next school year with the simple intention of just gracefully doing our best? Meaning, let's try our darndest to turn in every slip on time and remember every Wacky Hair Wednesday, all the while knowing that we'll inevitably forget something, be too busy to volunteer, or fail to compete with Liam's mom and her non-GMO custom gingerbread kits for every member of the class. Can we agree that imperfection is okay? Liam's mom is awesome at her thing—but you and me? We're awesome at ours. We can walk into the school year and remember that we're raising our children into the adults they will become. Our valiant endeavor will take us a lifetime of effort. A single day, or even a handful of days, when you aren't mom of the century won't make or break your kids. It's the intention to do well that will see them through. It's the lessons in grace and self-care and realistic expectations, where you teach them about what you're capable of, that will truly serve them later on. Choose a handful of things that you rock as a school mom, then knock those out of the park as often as you can. The other stuff? Give yourself the permission to do the best you can and the grace to be peaceful on the days when you miss the mark.

My children's attitudes will shift and grow over time. I believe that the very thing that makes me so different now—the company I run—is one of the things that will make me cool when they're older. I hope I'm creating something they'll be proud of. I hope I'm showing them the power of following their dreams and the value of entrepreneurship. I hope so many things for the future . . . but often those don't help me with today.

Today I am on yet another business trip, my third in as many weeks. Today Jackson is nervous about rehearsing his lines to audition for the class musical, and it's hard to accept because I'm good at musical theater but not there to help him. Today Ford has a cough and a fever, and he's been clingy and fighting us on bedtime. But I won't be there to help Dave manage him this evening around eight o'clock when he decides he's meant to stay up all night like a club promoter from the eighties.

There's always something.

Something that can overwhelm me and make me question whether or not I'm doing any of this correctly. That anxiety I felt when they were first born didn't exactly go away. It manifested and grew like a yeast starter. The only difference between now and then is that I'm better able to see that narrative for the lie that it is. Being a perfect mom is a myth—but being a pretty great mom, most of the time, is actually possible. I don't believe in one best way to parent. In fact, I think it could be pretty damaging to our children if we tried to impose the ideals of someone else onto how our family should function.

The Hollis boys are sarcastic. They get that from their parents. Dave and I think it's hilarious, and we admire their quick wit. But in your house, their sarcasm might be seen as disrespectful. Likewise, I'm incredibly strict with manners. I want *yes ma'ams* and *no sirs*. I demand *pleases* and *thank yous*, and if someone says something inappropriate or rude at my dinner table, they will be asked to leave. But maybe in your house that seems over the top. Maybe at your table you burp the alphabet after every meal and then laugh like maniacs together. If so, awesome. Mama, there is no one way to be a mother.

There's also no one way to be a family. Remember when I was talking to the new moms about the daily requirements: keep the baby alive, and keep yourself alive as well? Well, the list for older children might be extended, but the intention is still the same. You need to care, truly care that you are raising your babies to grow up to be good people. You need to do the work *today* to ensure that it happens. On some days you will knock it out of the ballpark, and on other days you will scream the house down, wondering who replaced your children with changelings who have horrible manners and no respect.

Good news! Tomorrow is a new day. Tomorrow you'll count to ten before you lose your temper, and maybe they'll eat every bite of the dinner you made and say something so hilarious you'll think, *Man, people without kids are totally missing out!* You will experience every kind of day as a mama, and you will need to accept the grab bag of good, bad, ugly, awesome, magical, and miserable days as a parent. You don't have to get it right all the time. You don't have to do things like anybody else's mom.

You only have to care.

Not only about them, but also about *yourself.* You cannot properly take care of your children or teach them how to be whole and happy people if you are miserable and harsh with yourself. That means doing the absolute best with them that you can. That means calling in reinforcements in the form of friends, your spouse, your mama, or the playland at your local gym when you're fraying at the edges and need a break. That means giving yourself time alone and away from the precious cherubs who are driving you crazy. Get a manicure, go for a run, or call up your college roommate for dinner. Better yet, plan a whole weekend if you can. Imagine two full days without once wiping anyone's nose. Imagine being called by your actual first name! Can you imagine sleeping in? Oh my gosh, girl, you are going to sleep *so* hard.

Or maybe you'll get a massage. Or maybe hole up somewhere all day watching Drew Barrymore movies on TBS . . . The world is your oyster! Then imagine coming home feeling uplifted and renewed, feeling better able to manage the squeals and screams and requests to have the crust cut off without wanting to lock yourself in the closet. Imagine living your motherhood out from now until forever, without guilt. Imagine caring for your children and yourself simultaneously without constantly questioning every decision you make. It's possible.

It's also a choice.

You have to choose not to compare. Don't compare your family to other families or yourself to other women or moms at school. You have to choose not to compare your children either—not to your friends' kids and most definitely not to each other. I am not saying that you shouldn't strive to improve yourself as a parent; and when it comes to kids, your job is to help them become their best selves. But sister, please, please, *please* stop allowing your fear of getting it wrong to color every beautiful thing you're doing right.

————

Years ago I had to make a choice. Either I had to embrace being a working mom and be wholly proud of what I was doing, or I had to quit and commit to being a stay-at-home mom. Constantly castigating myself for my choices wasn't fair to my children, and it definitely wasn't fair to me. I also wasn't setting a great example for them. Did I really want them to see me spending my life pursuing a dream while also anxiously acting as though I didn't deserve that right? Absolutely not.

A couple years ago, when I was trying to lose the baby weight from my second son, I went to visit my first trainer. She was a battle-ax of a woman with a fondness for burpees (clearly in league with the Devil), and more than once I puked after the time I spent with her. Jerk.

One day we were talking about my diet—at the time I was still going through a bad breakup with Carl's Jr.—and she asked me, "Would you ever feed your child the food you feed yourself?"

At the time I had a habit of going half a day without eating, then binging on anything and everything in sight. I was horrified by the question because I put so much time and energy into what my boys ate. No, of course I wouldn't ever feed my children the way I feed myself.

Later, a version of this question became the lifeline I used to pull myself back from the brink of debilitating mom guilt. Would I ever want my children to feel this way? Would I ever want them to pursue the desire of their heart, the profession that lights their soul on fire—be it a stay-at-home parent or cosmonaut or entrepreneur—but then constantly second-guess every choice they made because it doesn't look like everyone else's social media feed? Oh my gosh, you guys, the very idea makes my heart want to stop. I would never want them to struggle with their worth as I have. I would never want them to question themselves to the point of anxiety. I would never want them to think their entire parenting career could be summarily dismissed over Cheerios on a random school morning.

So I made a decision.

I will do my best, and I will trust that my best is exactly what God intended for these babies.

So I choose my battles. I do the best I can with the time I have, and I bend and stretch for the stuff that seems particularly important, even if it only makes sense in the mind of a seven-year-old. One season Sawyer announced that he only liked my sandwiches for lunch—not Daddy's. I started getting up early each day to make sure I was the only one who made their lunch. When Jackson told me he wanted to start running with me, I bought him shoes and went on the slowest mile-long jog the world has ever known. And when he told me I should get a necklace like the other moms . . . I got one.

I got that necklace, but there are still a hundred reasons why I don't fit into all of this as neatly as other women do. For example:

I hate organized sports.

Being a sports mom is sort of a badge of honor, right? Your kids get into soccer or baseball or hockey or gymnastics or whatever, and you jump right in along with them. All over Facebook and social media are pictures of mamas joyfully cheering from the sidelines. My girlfriend Kate recently told me she nearly lost her voice cheering at her son's game because she was so excited to be there. I love Kate for that: she is so quintessentially that sports mom who's in for every single part of it. But I am not.

I love my kids more than anything on this planet. But sports? Meh. Sports aren't really my thing. For several years I beat myself up because I dreaded having our Saturdays disrupted by a game schedule. I felt like a crappy mom because I *should* want to be out there watching my son play soccer or baseball, but I really didn't. Oh sure, on the outside I cheered and yelled and made the special game-day snacks, but on the inside—and *I know* I'll get flak for this admission—I thought (and still think) it's kind of boring.

My husband? He could not be more thrilled to be there. He loves sports of any kind, and I suspect watching his sons play them might be on his list of top three favorite things on this planet. But I don't get it. I mean, I'm happy the boys are happy. I'm thrilled that they're involved in a team sport, learning the benefits of physical activity and gaining confidence in themselves. Beyond that? It's just not my favorite thing. And I know there are those of you who don't understand this perspective. For you, these kinds of activities make your heart sing. For you, these kinds of moments are exactly what you imagined when you dreamed of being a mom—and I think it's so rad that you feel that way. It's awesome that we each get to experience moments of blissed-out mama pride with our babies, but what evokes that is different for every one of us.

If time has taught me anything, it's that our differences are what make this life unique. None of us are exactly like the other, and that is a good thing because *there's no right way to be.* The room mom, the working mother, the woman without children, the retired grandma, the mom who co-sleeps, the mama who bottle-fed her baby, the strict mom, the hipster mom, the one who lets her kid go shoeless, or the one who enrolls her baby in music enrichment classes at birth—whoever, *whatever* you are, you're adding spice and texture and nuance into this big beautiful soup of modern-day parenting. I can look at other mamas and learn from them. I can also leave the things that don't strike me as authentic or practical for *our* family. You can do the same for your own. That is the beauty of growing and learning and figuring out exactly who you are.

THINGS THAT HELPED ME . . .

1. *I looked at the evidence.* I used to spend so much time obsessing over all the things I was doing wrong as a mom. But you know what? My kids are awesome! Oh sure, they drive me bonkers at times, but they get great grades and are kind and welcoming to everyone they meet. I'm the one they come to when they're hurt. I'm the one they call out for in the night if they have a bad dream. Our bond is strong and unbreakable, which doesn't change simply because I'm a working mother. Look at the evidence in your own life. If you're raising arsonists who are rude to their grandma . . . well, maybe you need to seek out some help. But if your kids are basically good most of the time, then cut yourself some slack.

2. *I made friends with the other moms.* Yes, the ones your kids are comparing you to. Yes, the ones you're comparing yourself to. If they're at all human, then chances are they can tell you that they're also worried about screwing up their kids. Yes, Samantha's mom who sewed one hundred sequins onto one hundred buttons onto the hat she made by hand all to celebrate the one hundredth day of school? Yep. She's worried about her parenting too. The emperor has no clothes, y'all, and unless you seek out the truth, you're never going to know it.

3. *I focused on quality.* When I'm stressing about parenting, it's usually because I feel like I'm lacking for quality time with my kids. Quality time means I'm not on the phone or near a computer or talking to another adult. Usually it looks like reading, playing Candy Land, going on movie dates, or cooking with them. When I focus my energy on them, that's when I really feel content that I'm doing a good job.

CHAPTER 10

The Lie:

I SHOULD BE FURTHER ALONG BY NOW

Last week I sat around with a group of women enjoying a glass of wine and a chat. The women around me were all ages, came from different cities, and had various backgrounds. Some had families, some didn't, but all of them were what I would describe as successful. The topic of age came up and whether or not we liked to celebrate our birthdays and the passing of another year. The general consensus was *definitely not*.

This threw me for a loop.

I'm one of those people who loves her own birthday. I plan it months in advance and make long lists of things I want to do (wear sweatpants all day!) or what I want to eat (spinach artichoke dip with a funfetti cake for dessert!). I look forward to it with the same childlike glee as I did as a third grader. It's not just the actual celebration I like either; I wear each passing year with pride, and I truly don't care what age I am one way or another.

I know that women don't like growing older. That cliché has been around for as long as we've recorded history, I'm sure. But I had never really asked anyone why they felt that way. So I asked this group of ladies. I wanted to know what they disliked so much about growing older. The answer, at its core, was the same for every single person.

I expected some reference to looking older or even feeling older physically. I'd always assumed it had to do with lost youth, and maybe for certain people that's true. But this group's issue with passing time wasn't about what was happening.

They disliked growing older because of what *wasn't* happening.

You see, they'd all made plans. As little girls or adolescents or women in their early twenties, they'd made all sorts of them. Little plans and big plans and grandiose shoot-for-the-moon plans that they assumed would have been accomplished long before now. And while they had checked many things off their list, there were still those nagging few . . . the hanging chads of wishes and dreams that still hadn't come to fruition. So, for them, birthdays served as a reminder of all the things they *hadn't achieved*.

For some, they fell short of a career or financial goal. Others wanted to be married or have children. They had set themselves on some sort of course long ago, and each year they didn't reach that preconceived destination was a harsh reminder of the promises they were breaking to themselves.

Who hasn't fallen for this lie? I can't count the number of times in my life when I've beaten myself up because I thought my goals had expiration dates. (As a sidenote: What a downer attitude about a day that is supposed to be filled with buttercream icing!)

But, ladies, we need to recognize that this mentality doesn't do any of us any good. We're focusing all of our attention on the *absence* of something.

Imagine a little baby taking her first step. She's joyful and chubby and she's been balancing in place without holding on to the coffee table for weeks now. Finally, *finally*, she takes her first coltish stumble from the relative safety of the side table, then wobbles across the perils of the living room rug to grasp the edge of the sofa. She gets there and looks up at you with elation and pride and so much excitement. Now imagine you give her a quick, brittle smile and demand, "Yes, Chloe, that's fine, but why aren't you running by now?"

Can you imagine the dismay that baby girl would feel? What kind of parent has that kind of reaction to a child who's just learning to do something new? It would be unheard of for a mother to react so harshly, to judge a baby on what she hasn't yet had the time or life experience to figure out. And yet . . . and yet we do it to ourselves all the time.

Our own negative self-talk can be more damaging than the emotional abuse heaped on us by a hateful parent. It's also far more insidious because there's nobody there to stop it, since we rarely even realize it's happening. Beating ourselves up about all the things we think we're doing wrong becomes a litany of white noise. Eventually we don't even hear it anymore.

And for what? Because you thought you'd be partner at your firm by forty? Because you can't believe how much weight you've gained since having kids? Because your sister is already married and you're not even dating anyone? Because you dropped out of college and didn't get your degree? And you're thinking with every passing hour and day and week that it's too late?

I call bull crap.

God has perfect timing. If you aren't of a similar faith, think of it as everything happening exactly when it's supposed to. You look at your life and the eight things you thought you'd have accomplished by thirty-five and feel depressed. But maybe it's just that you don't have enough life experience yet. You're like the baby who's balancing in the middle of the room on chubby baby thighs—maybe you have to get your bearings for a while longer.

Or maybe that goal wasn't ever meant to be yours. Maybe you are destined for something so much cooler, which won't come until five years down the road. Maybe you have to walk through this space you're in to be ready for that. Nothing is wasted. Every single moment is preparing you for the next. But whether or not you choose to see this time as something wonderful—the time when God is stretching you and growing you or maybe forging you in fires hotter than you think you can withstand—all of it is growing you for the person you're becoming, for a future you can't even imagine.

When I decided to try and get pregnant for the first time, I thought I'd snap my fingers and be expecting the next minute. It took eight months to conceive. Eight months of hoping, eight months of crying every time I got my period, eight months of trying not to be jealous of the women around me who were pregnant, eight months of being sad when it didn't happen the way I thought it should.

The morning I finally took a test that showed me two pink lines, I ran over to the mirror to look at my face. I kept thinking, *I never want to forget how I looked when I found out I would be a mother.* I can still see myself in that mirror, wide-eyed and filled with shock and wonder.

Jackson Cage Hollis was born on January 30, 2007, and he is one of the greatest joys in my life. He loves computer games, cooking with me, and wears a stack of rainbow-colored rubber bracelets on his right wrist at all times because "they're cool, Mom, that's why." Guys, if I had gotten pregnant at any point during those eight months of trying, I wouldn't have had Jackson.

God has perfect timing.

I used to dream of being the biggest event planner in Los Angeles. I wanted a big staff and a fancy office and the highest-paying clients in town. Year after year I kept thinking, *This is the year I'll need a staff of twenty. This is the year I'll produce the Governor's Ball. This is the year I'll bring home a million dollars.* (I'm a dreamer, you'll recall.) And every year we grew but not as big as I hoped, and I'd feel so depressed that I wasn't as successful as I wanted to be.

Then my little blog—which was only ever supposed to be a marketing tool for the events company—started to grow a fan base, and I absolutely loved testing out recipes for them or talking about how to decorate a living room. Eventually the site became my full-time business, and a college dropout without any knowledge of tech or digital media found herself running a lifestyle media company with fans in the millions. Beyond that, this work is so much more fun and gratifying than the events ever were. If I'd had the biggest events company in LA with the staff and the millions, I wouldn't have had time to write the little blog that would eventually become my career and change the trajectory of my life completely.

God has perfect timing.

Dave and I walked through a long adoption journey. Nearly five years ago we started the process to adopt a little girl from Ethiopia. After mountains of paperwork and nearly a year of filing and preparing and getting fingerprints done for the hundredth time, we were officially vetted and waiting for a match.

Two years of waiting later, the adoption program in Ethiopia imploded and we found out that continuing to wait for a match was futile. We had to mourn the loss of the life, and the daughter, we had imagined for ourselves.

We started over. We decided to adopt through foster care in LA County because we recognized that the need was great. During that journey we took in two little girls through foster care, and I sobbed for weeks after they had to leave us. Two months later we got a call about newborn twin girls that would be ours. We brought them home from the hospital at six days old, we named them, and I experienced a love that can't properly be explained. Unbeknownst to us, their biological father decided he wanted them, and five weeks later the babies I thought were my daughters were taken back.

I wasn't sure how to think or feel, and I truly didn't know if I had it in me to try again for adoption. I knew I was letting my fear control me, that the worry about giving my heart away again only to have it stomped on kept me from taking a next step. In the midst of such heartache, it's hard not to worry. I cried so many tears, thinking, *Lord, why would you put this desire on my heart if it wasn't ever going to come true? And, God, if we try again, you're not actually sending my heart out to be slaughtered, right? Because this process with court dates and bio parents and doctor visits and trauma and the Department of Child and Family Services—that was already hard enough . . . You're not going to eviscerate us at the end of this, right? Right?!*

Amid these fearful thoughts, I heard him ask me, *Do you have faith in my plan or not?*

That is what it boils down to: faith. The belief that your life will unfold as it was meant to, even when it unfolds into something painful and difficult to navigate. Do I believe he has a plan?

Absolutely. I've seen the proof of it too many times to consider anything else. That means I have to hold on to that belief even when the process isn't simple or easy or safe.

I could make a list for you all day. I could point out a hundred different moments in my life when I thought I should have something and was so upset about not getting it, only to discover in retrospect that it wasn't ever meant to be mine. Looking back, I think that was the case with my daughter. The other girls were only meant to be ours for a little while—and for whatever reason, we were only meant to be theirs for a short time. We were a part of each other's journey, a stop along the way to the ultimate destination, even if we won't be there to see each other reach it.

As I sit editing this chapter, my daughter is asleep in a bouncy seat on the kitchen table next to my computer. Just five months after the twins left, five months after I could not imagine trying to adopt again, we were matched with her first-mom through independent adoption. That season was filled with anxiety. I was so terrified of the things that could go wrong—that *had* gone wrong in the past—that I could hardly function. But what came out of the experience was a relationship with both Noah and her first family that is so special it could only have been crafted by the divine. And yet again I am reminded that God has perfect timing.

If you have a goal, that's fantastic! I am one of the most motivated people you will ever meet, and my list of life goals is nine miles long. But I've learned that along with my list of goals, I have to give myself some grace. Being married by twenty-five, pregnant at thirty, and the president of my division before I turned forty are just arbitrary numbers. Because guess what? None of those preconceived notions or plans for myself worked out. Marriage and babies came way earlier than I thought . . . and career success came way later. Turns out, the most beautiful things in my life were never on my to-do list.

Today there may be items on your to-do list, but you also have a long list of things you *have* achieved. You've already done little things and big things . . . goals you accomplished years ago that are on someone else's bucket list. Focus on what you *have* done. Pay attention to the tiny steps you took across the living room carpet on wobbly legs. Celebrate the small moments. They're sacred, even if they aren't stepping stones to something else. Nothing is more important than today.

God has perfect timing, and it's highly possible that by not being where you thought you should be, you will end up exactly where you're meant to go.

THINGS THAT HELPED ME . . .

1. *Making a list.* Seriously. List out everything you've accomplished to date. In fact, write yourself a letter about your tenacity! I took a workshop with Elizabeth Gilbert last year, and she asked us to do this—to speak from the part of ourselves that has achieved so much, that refused to back down. You want to see a room full of people sobbing? Ask them to do this task. When you force yourself to admit to all the things you *have* accomplished, you'll realize that it's wrong to be so hard on yourself for all the things you haven't.

2. *Talking to someone.* Many times we don't admit to the way we're feeling because we're too embarrassed. But when you have someone you can talk to, who will listen to you say, "I feel worthless because I'm not a rock star by now," then you can experience the balm of their validation. "Are you kidding me

right now?!" they'll say. "Look at all the rad things you've done! You are amazing. Stop being so hard on yourself!" Remember, when you keep silent, you give those lies power.

3. *Setting goals, not time limits.* I love goals. They can help you become your best self . . . but big dreams shouldn't have expiration dates. As long as you're working toward the things you hope to accomplish, it shouldn't matter if it takes you a month or a decade.

CHAPTER *11*

The lie:

OTHER PEOPLE'S KIDS ARE SO MUCH CLEANER/BETTER ORGANIZED/MORE POLITE

I've spoken at my fair share of MOPS groups over the years, and I personally believe there will be a special place in heaven for anyone who has lived through the season of raising a preschooler.

Like with most talks I'm asked to give, I get the question about what I'd like to speak on when it comes to parenting. Sometimes they even have a theme for me to work with, such as "Better Together" or "A Journey into . . ."

On these occasions I try and work into the theme based on what I know well.

A Journey into the Left Side of the Taco Bell Menu . . .

A Journey into Books with a Vampire and Werewolf Love Triangle . . .

A Journey into Finally Learning the Cha-Cha Slide to Impress Your Kids Just Before the Whip/Nae Nae Brought You Back to Square One . . .

Inevitably I sit down and do my best to work up some thoughtful, poignant discussion based on the proposed theme. A Journey into Understanding the Gospel, perhaps? Or: A Journey into Finding Peace.

But when I try to sit down and write out my thoughts, I can't organize them . . . Life gets in the way, kids get in the way, work, bedtime, dinnertime, naptime . . . It all gets in the way.

I find myself thinking, *Lord! How do you expect me to speak about anything if I never get a moment's peace?! I'm running around here like my hair is on fire, and you're asking me to share wisdom with other women? You want me to talk about my faith?! I'm so tired I can't even spell* faith!

And I hear that still, small voice . . . *That is what I want you to speak about.*

This is probably the impetus for most if not all of the things I've ever done that resonated with other women and were therefore successful. I was struggling, and rather than try and sugarcoat it or pretend it wasn't happening, I simply acknowledged my struggles in my work.

So I am not going to talk about finding your peace; I'm going to talk about embracing your chaos. Let's be honest: this is way more likely a scenario because I don't know a woman alive today who can slow down long enough to find her keys, let alone a continuous state of inner peace. If you ever happened to find your peaceful inner bliss while raising children, please don't tell the rest of us. It'll only make us sad, and I eat raw cake batter when I'm sad.

I run a lifestyle media company that specializes in creating content for women. The tent pole of that company is the website, and every day a large fan base of ladies from all over the world checks in to figure out what to make for dinner or how to DIY a throw pillow or organize their kids for school or which outfits they should try for fall. I'm reminding you of that so you'll remember that I literally offer women advice for a living. Every single bit of the work I do is created to help make women's lives easier.

This is crucial because I'm about share an entire chapter on running toward chaos, on walking through hard things, on accepting the season you're in—even when it sucks. A decade of doing this job has taught me something, and I have a pretty strong theory. Ironically, I think embracing chaos might be the path to finding peace.

Have you ever heard of the chaos theory? Chaos theory is the field of study in mathematics that identifies the behavior and condition of dynamical systems that are highly sensitive to initial conditions—a response popularly referred to as the butterfly effect. FYI, I Googled that. I've never in my life written out a sentence with the words *dynamical systems* before or since this moment.

The butterfly effect is a long-ago term based on the idea that if you tracked the path of a hurricane from its inception, you'd find that it was all caused by a change in air pressure from the flap of a butterfly's wings three weeks prior and halfway across the world.

In simple terms, it just means that small things can have monstrous effects.

Chaos looks like: my three-year-old waking up at least once a night and battling to sleep in our bed; my website crashing and needing hours of repair; my brother-in-law making a trip to the hospital; my husband traveling for ten days on business; me getting hives or Bell's palsy or stress-induced vertigo; me spilling an entire gallon of milk; a bird pooping in my hair; a baby pooping in my hair; me fighting with my husband, my mom, my sister, or my husband's mom's sister . . . Y'all can fill in the blank with your own personal brand of chaos because we *all* have it.

Every single one of us is living in chaos, and we handle it in one of three ways:

1. **We ignore it.** This is one of my favorite methods of chaos management. I pretend it isn't there. I keep my head down and keep working harder and harder because nobody can hit a moving target.

   The problem with ignoring your chaos is that chaos by nature is incredibly stressful. It's like trying to pretend you're not really sick when you clearly have the flu. You can try to mind-over-matter it, but ultimately, stress always catches up to you, and your body will react in negative ways. For me, my stress has reacted with Bell's palsy or vertigo. My big sister gets hives when she's stressed out. Another friend gets insomnia. You may think it's not affecting you directly, but it *will* come out—and likely in ways that aren't healthy for you or your family.

2. **We battle it.** Typically we battle chaos on a completely different field from the one we really need to address. So, in response to our relationships being stressful, we might clean the kitchen. We'll clean the bedroom and the front room. We clean the kitchen again. We brush our kids' hair and wipe their faces and cry when they get ketchup on their church clothes. We do

everything in our power to have a picture-perfect existence, because maybe then the inside will match the outside.

The problem with a battle is that we will always lose. If we believe we can do enough or organize enough or plan enough to make sure that nothing is ever difficult, we will only make ourselves feel like a failure when life is too hard. Life is crazy and stressful, and sometimes it gets worse before it gets better. Losing a battle against regular, everyday life makes us feel impotent and angry. It makes us feel out of control.

3. *We drown in it.* We get overwhelmed by housework, regular work, family, and friends. The stressful things become all we see. It feels insurmountable—and no matter what we do, it doesn't get better. We slip into wallowing. We complain, we crawl under the covers, and we let the chaos win.

The problem is, drowning means suffocating. And if we choose to stay underwater without kicking our way to the surface, we eventually forget how to swim.

Sister, you are stronger than this. You've got babies to raise and bills to pay and a life to live—and you can't do that if you're hiding under the covers!

Also, each of these ways—avoiding, battling, and drowning—is a prime platform for the false life preserver of substance abuse. You can use food to avoid facing your life. You can get drunk as a way to drown your sorrows. You can reach for so many negative substances to take your mind away from the chaos around you—and many of us do so without realizing that we're developing a dangerous, regular coping mechanism instead of a one-time escape.

The biggest problem with all three of those things? Any one

of them implies that you are the one in control. And to some extent that's true . . . after all, the driving force behind this book is to remind you that you are in control *of yourself.* But you cannot control the actions of others, your kids having a meltdown, the baby having a blowout at Target, the dog digging up your yard, or the washing machine breaking down. And when you think you can, you'll only find yourself angry, frustrated, and stressed. Also, when you assume you're in total control, you don't stop and take time to seek out a relationship with God; you use alternative means to try and manufacture some peace.

So what are our options? Ignore it, battle it, medicate the chaos until we feel numb to its effects? No way, we are stronger than that, even if it's hard to feel it when you're buried under a pile of laundry and a horde of hyper children.

There is another option—one people rarely cling to—embrace the madness. Interestingly enough, the people I know who do this best are the ones whose lives are the most chaotic of all. They're my friends whose husbands are serving overseas. They're the women I know who are raising special-needs children. They're the single mamas working three jobs. I believe it's because they learned a long time ago that there is beauty in the chaos, as well as freedom in not trying to fight against the tide.

The thing is, Jesus was the ultimate embracer of chaos. He preached and taught and shepherded a flock, and in the midst of his tumultuous ministry, he accepted *everyone.* Everyone was allowed to join in on the love. The widows, the prostitutes, the lepers, the orphans, people with great need, people who brought drama and stress into his life, and folks who weren't always lovable or even kind. Furthermore, Jesus told us to love them too. He didn't ask us kindly or say, "Hey guys, maybe you could . . ." No, he straight up called us to stand with the oppressed. Jesus looked at them and said, "Bring it on." Jesus took in the messy, broken pieces and said, "Behold, I am making all things new" (Rev. 21:5 WEB). Amid our chaos, fear, and frustration there is the reminder, "For *everything* there is a season, and a time to every purpose under heaven" (Eccl. 3:1 WEB, emphasis added).

You're sitting in your house, in your neighborhood, in your city, and thinking, *This is so hard. Nobody else understands. I can't keep up. Blah, blah, blah.* And God is up there like, *Good and perfect daughter, I have been talking about this since Jump Street!*

Being overwhelmed isn't a new concept.

Having a tough day or week? Do you snap at your husband or want to pull your hair out? You haven't cornered the market on that. You are not the only one. The way you deal with your stress, though, is where your individuality comes through.

So maybe you're reading this and you're thinking, *Okay, I'm in . . . I get it. Let's embrace this chaotic life! But how in the heck do I do that?*

Start by giving yourself some grace. We all mess up; we all make mistakes; we all forget pajama day or mix it up with picture day. I've screamed at my kids, my husband, and myself. None of it feels good, all of it devastates me, because the loss of control is so upsetting. But you know what? Tomorrow is another day and a chance to try again.

Take a breath. Find humor in the situation, and force yourself to look for it when it's not immediately evident. A couple of years ago when we were getting certified to be foster parents, a social worker had to interview each of our kids. We sat in the living room with them while she asked innocuous questions over iced tea. She gave them harmless prompts . . . harmless until she spoke to a barely four-year-old Ford Hollis.

"What makes you happy?" she asked.

He said he liked to go swimming.

"And what makes you sad?" she followed up.

Without hesitation he told her, "When Daddy scares me in the night."

Both Dave and I froze like deer in headlights. What? What the heck was he talking about? And why was he choosing right now, with a social worker from Child Protective Services, to work through this?

"What do you mean when Daddy scares you in the night?"

"You know, when he comes to my room in the night and he's mad at me."

Y'all, when you do an interview like this, you're already on edge; but when your kids say something crazy, you think that not only are you not going to get approved for foster care but also you might lose the children you *do* have.

More questions revealed that Ford was talking about the night before when he'd woken up in the middle of the night and tried to sneak in bed with us (which is against the rules). Daddy was grouchy when he had to walk him back to bed three times at two o'clock in the morning. It's hilarious in hindsight, but at the time, before we'd gotten clarification, I thought I was going to hyperventilate. So push yourself to laugh at hard situations. In fact, the crazier the situation, the more humor you should be able to mine from it.

I also encourage myself, and you, to look for the fruits of the Spirit. For those of you who didn't grow up singing them on a kids' worship music tape before breakfast each morning like I did, the fruits of the Spirit are love, joy, patience, peace, kindness, goodness, faithfulness, gentleness, and self-control. All of these are incredible values, but I believe there's always one that we need the most in a particular season. Choose the one that resonates with you at this moment, write it down on some Post-its, and stick them everywhere.

Don't forget to take a break, take care of yourself, go on a date, or get your nails done. Take some time just for you to refill your cup, and you'll be better able to embrace all the madness when you step back inside of it.

Find a tribe of people who are in a similar walk of life as you are. Once you find them, be honest about where you are and what you're struggling with. Learn to ask for help, and when someone offers help, accept it! Accept any and all help you can get and consider it a gift from God! I cannot tell you how many women ask me how I "do it all," and when I tell them that I've learned to ask for help, they look at me as if I'm an alien.

"Like, help with what?"

For example, when your mother-in-law says she'll come for the afternoon and entertain the kids, say, "Yes, please." If your husband offers to fold the laundry (even when you don't think he's good at folding towels), say, "Yes, please." If your girlfriend says she wants to bring you dinner or wine but you feel bad that you're putting her out, say, "Yes, please." Or if your elementary school offers afternoon classes that will occupy your rambunctious boys for an additional hour and a half, say, "Yes, please."

What can give you more time, more space, more freedom to find your center? Whatever it is, say, "Yes, please" to that!

Remember that old joke about how a man keeps praying for God to save him from drowning? Someone comes by in a boat and asks him if he needs a ride, and he's like, "Nah, God will save me." When it happens two more times, he says the same thing both times. Spoiler alert: The man ends up drowning, and when he gets to heaven, he's like, "God, what the heck? I asked you to save me." And God looks at him and says, "Dude, I sent you three different life rafts, and you ignored each one."

Girlfriend, God is sending you all kinds of life rafts. Some are big and obvious, and some are as simple as the bagger at the store offering to load your groceries into your car. Get in the freaking boat!

Remember Philippians 1:6: "Being confident of this, that he who began a good work in you will carry it on to completion." Oh man, I just love that scripture. I believe it's true, and I've watched it unfold in my life again and again. You will get through this season. This too shall pass. Don't set the rest of your life up on a downhill slope because of one hard season.

It also might be helpful to remember that someone else is praying to have the kind of chaos you're currently crying about. What I mean is, the things you think are so difficult could be someone else's dream come true. I don't say that to make you feel bad, or to negate your difficult experience; but perspective may help you see that your chaos is actually just a gigantic blessing. Adjusting your view can work wonders.

Lastly, remember the butterfly effect? Well, let's consider an actual butterfly, or more specifically, a caterpillar. Caterpillars are awesome. They have all those legs and they're really cool, and there's an entire children's book series about how pretty they are. But if the caterpillar just chose to stay a caterpillar, if she decided that the chaos of metamorphosis would be too much for her to handle, she would never know what she could become. Do you think that changing her entire being isn't painful? Do you think it's not scary and hard and overwhelming? Of course it is, but if she didn't fight against the fear, if she didn't allow the change to turn her into her true self, we would never know how beautiful she is. She would never know that she was meant to fly.

THINGS THAT HELPED ME . . .

1. *Friends like me.* Meaning, friends who were newly married when I was newly married. Friends who are entrepreneurs because I'm an entrepreneur. Friends who are working moms or boy moms or have kids at similar ages . . . they're all lifesavers. Having someone you can grab a glass of wine with who can totally relate to your day is a gift. Such friends are vital in helping me feel encouraged.

2. *Priorities.* You can keep a clean house or start a company or stay at home with a baby or build a slammin' bod from working out seven days a week . . . but I don't think you can have all of those at the same time, or at least not in the same increments. Sit down and decide what's really important to you. Not what's important to your mother-in-law or your girlfriends . . . Decide what's really important to *you*. Then do those things first. If the house is cluttered or you need to wait until next year to train for a half marathon, well, that's just life.

3. *Boxed wine.* Okay, I'm kidding. Well, slightly kidding. I do think you should have something that helps you unwind. Running or watching HGTV or baking might be the thing for you. No matter what, find something in your life that feels like a treat or an indulgence. When you're feeling extra frazzled, you should be able to go to your happy place and reset.

CHAPTER 12

The Lie:

I NEED TO MAKE MYSELF SMALLER

I went to a conference last year—the kind of thing where a life guru stands on stage and walks you through guided meditation or yells at you to believe in yourself.

I loved every single second of it.

As I constantly analyze how I can grow and become a better version of myself, I appreciate wisdom wherever I can get it. No one person can be your source for all the answers, but you can glean a handful of powerful thoughts here and a dash of insight there. I hope you get some great tangible advice from me, but I don't for one moment believe that you're going to take every single thing in these pages as gospel.

So I read the books and listen to the podcasts, and when

GIRL, WASH YOUR FACE

someone I admire fills an arena nearby for a few days of wisdom, you better believe I'm buying a ticket. It was during an experience like this that I had a powerful insight into something about myself I never expected.

"Which parent did you crave love from more?" the speaker asked the crowd. "Not which parent did you love more . . . Which one did you *crave love* from more?"

My dad.

I would assume that this is true for many women, but it's definitely the truth for me. And here's the thing: I've done a lot of therapy, and much of it was so I could work through questions like this one. So when he asked the audience whom we craved love from the most, my answer was my dad. But, *I already knew that*, no great surprise there.

Then he asked the follow-up question that changed everything.

"And who did you have to *be* for them?"

Meaning, what did you believe as a child that you needed to do to receive that parent's love?

"Successful," I grumbled to myself. This was not news to me. As I've already mentioned, I understood all about how being a "performer" had affected my life as an adult.

"Besides that," the man on stage asked, "what else did you have to be?"

"Small."

It fell out of my mouth without conscious thought. Before that moment, I can tell you I had never, ever considered that concept before.

Where did that come from? What did I even mean by it?

I sat back in my chair and considered it for the first time in my life.

I believe my father was always proud of me, but he wasn't

verbal with that praise unless I did something well. As a hard worker himself, he appreciated the achievement. Simultaneously, because he'd never had a great example of what it meant to be a good dad, he had nothing to go by. He had no idea what to do with little kids. My memory is that as children, we understood we should be seen and not heard. I learned quickly not to make a fuss—not to make noise at all if it wasn't what he wanted. Sometimes he wanted to interact, to have conversations or even play. But most of the time he wanted silence.

As I got older I was aware of the disparity more and more.

Little girl.

That was what he called me . . . and not as an endearment.

Little girl, you have no clue what you're talking about.

Little girl, the real world is going to eat you alive.

Little girl, you'd better grow up quick.

Little girl became an expletive. I *hated* when he called me that but never truly understood how it affected me before that day at the conference. And not just negatively, but positively as well. I wouldn't be who I am were it not for my childhood. I wouldn't be *where* I am without the work ethic instilled in me by my father. The same man who praised my achievement might have unintentionally taught me to chase it a bit too much, but you can't blame the past for the things that went wrong if you aren't also willing to be thankful for the things that went right. Digging into the *whys* of how I behave as an adult are what make me able to overcome unhealthy habits.

Take, for example, how uncomfortable I used to become when speaking about my job. If you asked me at a party what I did for a living, I'd say something dismissive like, "Oh, I have a lifestyle blog." Never mind the fact that I built a media company from the ground up and manage a staff of eleven. Never mind that our clients are some of the biggest brands on earth. Never mind that the website gets millions of visitors a month or that I'm an author and public speaker while also raising babies. It feels boastful to mention those things; it feels like I might make you uncomfortable if I speak about them.

A larger part of why I don't want to be boastful is because I learned a long time ago that I was a little girl who had no clue what she was talking about. Being big while also being small is an impossible task for anyone. As I sat at the conference that day, I understood how that dilemma had colored so much of who I had become.

As a company we have been offered so many large opportunities over the last few years, and I'd found one excuse after another to turn them down. I worried that we would disappoint our clients. I worried that we would fail. I worried that I wasn't smart enough to lead the team into new territory.

It's hard to write it down now because I spend so much time telling other women to chase their big dreams. And if you had asked me, *of course* I would have told you that we were daring ourselves to grow by leaps and bounds. But when I took a real look at my life and my company, I recognized the truth: I was making myself small. I was performing just enough to gain your attention but not truly being myself for fear of what everyone might think of the real me.

Who am I really?

I'm a wife and a mother, and I also dream of being a true media mogul. I am working to grow my lifestyle media agency to incredible heights. I dream of having enough revenue so that all of these incredible people who work for me—who took a chance on helping with *my dream*—can own their own homes, pay off their student loans, and take long, dreamy vacations somewhere sunny. I dream of starting a nonprofit that supports other women who want to chase down dreams of their own. I'm working to build a company my children will grow up and work at too. I think the media we consume can positively impact our lives, and by creating media that uplifts and encourages women, we can literally change the world.

I have so many goals and dreams for myself, and not one of them is small. They're big and wild and full of hope. They require faith and courage and a whole lot of audacity. I cannot get there, I *will not* get there, unless I start embracing every side of my character—including the sides of me that make other people uncomfortable.

This is what occurred to me at the conference that day: I cannot continue to live as half of myself simply because it's hard for others to handle all of me.

I was at another conference just a few weeks ago when I saw this playing out in other women around me. Four hundred inspiring, entrepreneurial-minded women, and I kept hearing them saying the same things over and over:

"Well, this is just my hobby."
"This is just something I do on the side."
"My job is being a mom, but this is a great side gig."

Y'all, these were not women casually selling antiques from their garage on Etsy. These women were running businesses and teams. Some of them were making hundreds of thousands of dollars a year, yet I heard the word *hobby* over and over.

It made me realize: I am not the only woman who is making herself small to make others feel more comfortable.

It's hard for people who don't understand us to be fully

supportive. When you boil it down, that's the heart of the problem with my father. He couldn't understand what to do with a small child, let alone a girl. Since he didn't understand me, he often unintentionally muted the parts of me that made him uncomfortable.

Working women sometimes have to fight their way through patriarchal systems. Working mothers get backlash from in-laws or parents who can't understand our desire to work, while stay-at-home moms slam us for being away from our children. I'll bet stay-at-home moms feel similarly judged by working women who can't relate to their life choices. It's as though we're all children on a playground trying to say whatever others want to hear, trying to hide all the parts that others might not understand. It makes me wonder how many women are walking around living in half their personality and in doing so, denying who their Creator made them to be.

Do you really think God made you—uniquely, wonderful you—in hopes you would deny your true self because it might be off-putting to others? I can't believe that's true. The more I've thought about it, the more I believe that God made me this way. He knew I would have a worker's heart, and he knew I would want to build big dreams. In the same way, he knew another one of his children was meant to stay home and raise her beautiful babies, while another daughter of his wouldn't want to have kids at all.

Have you spent a lifetime muting yourself for fear of what others will think? Are you an entrepreneur who calls your business a hobby because you worry about what your mother-in-law will say or because it's safer to keep everyone's expectations low? Are you hesitating to go back to school because you think you're not smart enough? Do you stop yourself from daring to try something new because you're already positive you'll fail? Do you remain silent when you have so much to say? Do you believe you'll never do better or be better than you are right now because of your family of origin? Do you hesitate to admit your dreams aloud because you're nervous about others making fun of you or judging you for your choices?

Girl.

I lived in fear of this for years. I worried that if you knew how much I love to work you might call into question how I can do any of those things while being a successful mother. I've had too many people question my commitment to my children over the last ten years, and it influenced what I came to believe about being a working woman. It was a long battle from mommy guilt to acceptance, and I was only ever able to work through it after we adopted our daughter. When she was about six weeks old, I had to go on a business trip; and while I was gone someone asked me about mommy guilt as a working mom. It's a question that comes up a lot and one that I bet most mothers—regardless of whether they stay home with their babes or choose to work—have grappled with.

I've thought about it a lot over the last ten years of motherhood, and even more so now that I'm raising a daughter.

And here's what I've decided . . .

I *refuse* to teach her this narrative.

I absolutely refuse to raise her with the ideal that only one parent is ultimately responsible for who she will become. I was raised by two working parents and the proverbial village.

I will not consent to the belief that having a mother with a full-time job means that she's not loved and well cared for.

I will not set her up to believe that having a career (or not) has *anything* to do with how much she's committed to her partner or how much she loves her children . . . should she choose to have either.

I will not tell her that a man's work is only out in the world or that a woman's work is inside the home. If she *chooses* to stay at home, then we will support her with all our hearts; but we will never teach her that there's only one kind of woman to be.

This is important because her brothers will be told by society that their options are endless, and she will be shown by media that her world is limited.

I know this for many reasons, but mostly because her daddy has never *one time* been asked if he feels guilty for having a job.

As she grows, my daughter will learn things out in the world that I wish she didn't—I cannot control that—but I *can* control the kind of woman I set as an example. I, her mother, believe that Noah, my daughter, is fearfully and wonderfully made by a God who imagined her place in this world long before either of us was born.

I believe the same thing about you.

I believe that you are not a mistake—and feeling guilt about who you are (working, staying at home, overweight, underweight, overeducated, uneducated, emotional, bookish, street-smart, or whatever) does a disservice to yourself and the Creator who made you.

There are hundreds of ways to lose yourself, but the easiest of them all is refusing to acknowledge who you truly are in the first place.

You—the *real* you—is not an accident.

Those dreams you have for yourself are not silly; they are the road map to your divine calling! Don't sit this one out. Don't let someone else's opinion of you determine your worth. Don't miss out on the chance to live the life of incredible possibility in front of you.

You were not made to be small.

You are not a little girl.

You are a grown woman, and it's time you grew up. Become exactly who God calls you to be.

THINGS THAT HELPED ME . . .

1. *A willingness to offend.* I don't mean *offend* as in "tell a bunch of *yo mama* jokes." I mean embrace the idea that not everyone can understand or approve of you, including those closest to you. If you're a people-pleaser like I was, this is especially hard because my instinct is to ensure that everyone likes me at all times. So I decided to get out of my own way and stop focusing so much on what anyone else thought. I focus on being the best, most loving version of myself—but whether or not you approve of that isn't my concern.

2. *A bold statement.* For me, it was a tattoo. I'd secretly wanted one for years, but I was worried about what others would think. Then I had an epiphany: *I get to decide who I am.* Every single day we're alive, we're choosing this life and this persona. We choose to be the stay-at-home mom who loves baking and Pilates. We choose to be a hipster who loves coffee shops and artisan goods. We choose to be a lawyer who runs marathons and only eats organic. Every single aspect of our persona, no matter how long we've rocked it, is a choice we make every day. This was a *massive* eye-opener for me. And as odd as it sounds, when I realized this and it hit me right between the eyes, the very first thought I had was, *I'm getting a wrist tattoo!*

3. *An encounter with a guru.* Many times I need the insight of a podcast, a book, or a conference to gain perspective. If

you wonder if you are muting a side of yourself, or if there are things you know you want to work on, start consuming content that speaks to that specific area. You may not adopt every word of what you hear or read, but you'll certainly garner a bit of wisdom to help you with your season.

CHAPTER 13

The Lie:

I'M GOING TO MARRY MATT DAMON

Laugh all you want, but this was something I believed for *years*. I've talked about my obsession with Matt Damon many times, mostly because it's funny and I live to make other people chuckle. It's also an easy laugh because people have a hard time reconciling a seemingly intelligent, sane person believing that she will marry a celebrity she's never met. But the truth is, there was a time—whole years of my life, in fact—when my greatest life plan was to find Matt Damon somewhere in LA and lock it in.

I spent most of my junior year in high school watching *Good Will Hunting* over and over. I can still recite the entire movie for you by heart if you need me to. I applied over and over again for jobs at Miramax Films (because they had produced *Good*

Will Hunting and my eighteen-year-old brain assumed that Matt Damon might stroll through the lobby at any given moment). For my last year living at home and my first year in Los Angeles, this fantasy of Matt as my knight in shining armor kept me going. I imagined it in vivid detail: how we'd meet, what I'd wear, where we'd marry, what our house would look like, what our kids would look like . . . When I found myself in a bleak place, those imaginings were the light at the end of my tunnel. I truly believed they were where I was headed.

When I finally did bump into Matt while working a party for Miramax a year into working there, he walked right toward me at the back of the theater. I mean, hand to dog, he made a beeline for where I was standing. My heart nearly exploded in my chest because it was happening exactly the way I thought it would. He saw me and somehow just knew we were destined to be together. As soon as he got within earshot, he started to speak.

"Excuse me," he said.

This is it! I thought.

"Do you know where I'm supposed to sit?"

He spoke to me because he was a celebrity and I was the girl with the clipboard in her hands—not because he sensed we were destined to be together. I walked him to his assigned spot and left him there without a marriage proposal or even a request for a date.

After living in LA for a year, enough reality had hit me to understand that my former imaginings were part of a childish daydream.

Later on in life I had another fantasy. This one was smaller, the outcome less life-altering, but I obsessed about it almost as much.

I wanted a Louis Vuitton bag.

More specifically, I wanted a Louis Vuitton *Speedy* bag.

For those of you who aren't familiar, it's one of LV's classics. It's about the size of a regulation football, and at the time they cost a little over a thousand dollars.

One. Thousand. Dollars. For a bag the size of my head.

It was ridiculous, but I still wanted it. I wanted it because it represented the kind of woman I dreamed of becoming.

During my first summer living in LA, I often visited the Beverly Center. The Beverly Center is a fancy-pants mall in Beverly Hills, and at the time I couldn't afford anything other than the six dollars it took to park there. Even still I would wander around window-shopping and dreaming of someday. It was on one such trip when I saw the most glamorous woman I'd ever seen—or at least, the epitome of what I hoped to look like someday. Her hair was glossy, her makeup was perfect, her outfit was cute, and in her hand she carried a Louis Vuitton Speedy bag. Even better? She'd tied a vintage scarf around the handle of that bag, making it the classiest-looking thing I'd ever witnessed in real life. In that moment I was sold on this ideal. Someday I was going to be as pulled together and stylish as that woman. Someday I was going to own that bag.

I coveted it for years knowing it was a total fantasy. A thousand dollars was an astronomical sum to spend on something so frivolous, but I still imagined what I'd do with that bag. I imagined where I'd use it and how I'd change out the scarf seasonally or to match my outfit. I pictured it in great detail, and over time I came up with a game plan for achieving it. Someday I would build a company, and someday that company would have real clients who would pay me really big money. The first time someone gave me a check for $10,000 in consultation fees, I decided I was going to buy myself that bag.

It took me years, you guys.

Years of scraping and hustling as a small-time wedding planner. Years of building up my portfolio of work and my client roster. Years of charging $750, then $1,000, then more. Every time I went to the mall I'd walk by Louis Vuitton and stare at that bag through the window. Through every meeting and contract, I held on to that vision. For every mean bridezilla or drunk best man speech or late night cleaning confetti out of the hotel carpet so my clients wouldn't lose their deposit, I kept thinking, *I'm going to get that Speedy bag!*

The day I received my first $10,000 check, I drove directly to the bank—and then from the bank to the Louis Vuitton store at the Beverly Center. When I walked out of that store it was the proudest I'd ever been in my whole life.

A purse is cool, and a Matt Damon obsession is . . . er, *interesting*, perhaps. But why bring them up now? Why tell you about this random quirky lie or this purse I used to be obsessed with when the other chapters carry so much weight and seriousness?

Because I think my ability to imagine my dreams in intricate detail is one of the biggest reasons I've been able to achieve them. Seriously. Don't rush by that statement. Sit with it for a minute. A huge part of my success is built into my imagination. And I don't mean Tim Burton–style imagination. I just mean the ability to pick out a daydream and then focus on it . . . sometimes for years.

One of the questions I get most often is how I stay motivated. Lately I've been trying to offer tangible ideas: surround yourself with inspiring people (both in real life and in your social media feeds); listen to motivational podcasts; blast pump-up jams until you're feeling inspired; figure out a formula for what motivates you, then do it again and again. But that may sound like advice you've probably heard before, so what's the point of repeating information that won't stick? I'd rather hone in on what's going to make the big difference for you, even if it might sound a little strange. For me, the big difference was envisioning a very specific future.

Believing I would marry Matt Damon was borderline crazy . . . but it got me to LA, and it led me to fighting for and getting a job at Miramax Films, which then led me to both my career as an event planner and my future husband. In the absence of clear direction or a real vision, I just imagined one. I latched on to the idea of a future so I knew a direction to walk in. Along the way I grew up and learned about my destination, but had I not held that idea in my head, who knows where I would have gone—or more importantly, how I would have mentally escaped the hard times while I was still inside of them. When I was dreaming about that purse, my larger goals of making a decent salary and contributing to the bank account I shared with my new husband seemed over-whelming. They didn't feel tangible.

But breaking it down into a bite-sized goal—in my case, buy-ing a purse—was achievable. Calling your shot is powerful when you're chasing down a dream, but it's also not enough. You have to spend real time focusing on everything you can about that dream. What does it look like? What does it feel like? How much detail can you imagine? How real can you make it in your own mind? Because here's the deal: my goals are real to me. There isn't a single doubt or question in my mind that I can achieve them. I have absolute certainty—the same way I did with Matt or that ridiculously expensive handbag. Whether or not the dream ulti-mately comes true isn't the point; the point is, how do you steer your ship in a clear direction? How do you stay on course even when the water is choppy or the boat is crashing on rocks? You do that by keeping your eyes on the horizon.

For me, my daydreams were an attempt to keep my eyes above the waves. When life was hard and murky and difficult to navigate, having a clear vision gave me something to focus on. I can't recommend it enough for you.

Do you have a goal for yourself? I'll tell you again: write it down. No, seriously. Write. It. Down! Imagine it in intricate detail. Focus on it whenever you can. What will it feel like to get healthy? How will your clothes fit? Or how about your dream job? What will your first day at that company be like? How about the fiftieth day? What will you be able to do in your free time because you have that position? How much happier will you be? I like visuals as well. I keep my visual reminders of my current goals taped up inside my closet so every single time I get dressed (which is daily, yo) I see them as a reminder.

What are they?

I knew you'd ask.

One is the cover of *Forbes* with the top female self-made millionaires. The second is a picture of a vacation home in Hawaii. Both have been on my wish list for years . . . the house in particular feels extra dreamy but hard to achieve. My goal is to own it by the time I'm forty . . . so I've got five years.

You guys, I can't tell you how often I've felt tired or discouraged or *whatever*, and I've closed my eyes and imagined my fortieth birthday party at the house in Hawaii that I've dreamed up. My friends, my kids, my husband, and my family are there, and we're all drinking some fabulous cocktail. I'm wearing a gorgeous caftan of some kind . . . because when you make enough to buy your own Hawaiian vacation home, you can wear whatever you want and there's *no way* I'm restricting my midsection. That birthday party and that house are crystal clear in my mind; they help me focus when I get bogged down.

Sometimes these daydreams work as a distraction technique too.

When I'm running long distance or training for a race, my imagination is a stellar tool for focusing on something else. Back when I trained for my first half marathon, my only goal was just to finish without dying. The next time around, the goal was to run those thirteen miles faster than I did the time before. That meant training often and well, doing long runs and tempo runs, and pushing myself each time. It's hard, y'all, and it hurt muscles I hadn't used since I did step aerobics back in the nineties!

When I run I use this trick for getting through any strenuous workout—and you are free to use it too. It's utterly ridiculous, and even a little embarrassing, but it works for me *every time.*

I believe Mindy Kaling coined the phrase *cardio fantasies*— how she invents stories to entertain herself as she exercises. If she didn't, someone please trademark that for me and I'll turn it into my next book and a line of activewear.

My cardio fantasy is the big, crazy dream I typically imagine myself in during a particularly difficult workout. Sometimes the music in my headphones can get me through, but when the going gets tough, the tough (me in this scenario) imagines herself vacationing with George Clooney at his house in Lake Como.

Laugh at me all you want, but I've found that the more outlandish the cardio fantasy, the more time I can pass without noticing that my quads are screaming.

Don't have your own cardio fantasy? Borrow one of mine. These are (no, seriously) my go-tos. You think I'm trying to be funny here, but I swear by the power of Grayskull, these are really what I'm thinking about:

Best Friends with Your Hero. As you may or may not know, I am the biggest book nerd you've ever met in your whole life. Don't even start a book conversation with me unless you really want to take it to level five, because I will embarrass myself. There's no author on earth I want to meet more than Deborah Harkness. Because I'm a super nerd, I also know that she lives relatively near-ish my weekly running spot. I like to imagine a detailed scenario where she's on the same trail I am and I recognize her and we basically become best friends and meet weekly to walk and discuss the intricate plot points of her next book.

Vacationing with Celebrities. I wasn't kidding about the George Clooney thing. I like to imagine I'm part of a large collection of celebrity couples and we're all vacationing somewhere amazing. In this same scenario my hair is always shiny and my makeup a dewy J.Lo-like special. I make everyone dinner and surprisingly, even the super-skinny movie stars like meatloaf and casseroles. They ask where they can get my cookbook, and they all love me because, for a billionaire media mogul, I'm surprisingly down-to-earth.

Singing on Stage with Lionel Richie. I have a lot of Lionel Richie on my iPod, so this was sort of a forced fantasy. At some big birthday party of mine (that fortieth in Hawaii, let's say), Lionel is a longtime family friend who surprises me by coming to perform. At some point he pulls me up on stage and we sing together . . . I can't actually sing well in real life, but in this scenario I *crush* "Dancing on the Ceiling." Later, as an encore, we do a haunting duet of "Hello," and years later friends will still recall, "Geez, Rachel, do you remember that one time you and Lionel sang 'Hello'?"

Ryan Gosling or a Hemsworth Brother. I'm far too much of a weenie to have any real fantasies about these guys, but I do like dreaming about some situation where I look flawless and am so totally hilarious and witty that one of these stallions can't help but hit on me. Propriety forces me to tell Ryan/ Chris/Liam that I'm happily married, but the dream of them asking will still be with me when I'm ninety years old.

Some fantasies are instrumental in helping us reach our goals. Some fantasies are silly, but they give us something to think about. If you ask me, all of them have value. And your fantasies will be different from mine! Maybe you cure a rare disease or have dinner with Oprah. Maybe you talk politics with Roosevelt or try on dresses with Edith Head. The point is, you don't think about the challenge before you; you keep your eyes above the waves.

So stop laughing at my nerdiness and find whatever motivation you need to get out there today and make some moves.

THINGS THAT HELPED ME . . .

1. *Writing it down.* I cannot stress this enough: when it comes to goal setting, it's imperative that you write everything down. Okay, maybe not your Matt Damon–related goals (I was a teenager, you guys!), but if you're dreaming of something for yourself, physically writing down the words is a powerful thing to do.

2. *Saying it aloud.* Naming your goals is also important, because often we struggle to even admit them to ourselves. Make sure when you name yours, you do it in a powerful way. Say, "I am getting my master's in organizational psychology" instead of "I will try to go back to school." I drive around town saying my goals in my car where no one can hear me. I announce them like proclamations . . . as if it's only a matter of time before they happen.

3. **Creating a vision board.** The pictures inside my closet hold a lot of meaning for me. They're a constant reminder of where I want to go, and a visual aid can be really helpful for those of you who don't feel like your imagination is strong. Use someone else's visuals to help you map out your dreams in your mind.

CHAPTER 14

The lie:

I'M A TERRIBLE WRITER

After I published my first book, *Party Girl*, I would occasionally (read: every eleven seconds) check Goodreads to see what people were saying about it. As a massive book nerd who devours online reviews in order to build my TBR pile, it felt *so* exciting to read other people's reviews of *a book I had written!* It was such an incredible boost for me—especially as I fought my way through writing the sequel—to see the lovely things readers were saying. I was driven to tears more than once by some sweet fan explaining exactly why she loved my characters, all as I'm thinking, *Yes! That is exactly what I hoped you'd see in her!* I lived in this dream world for months. I honestly didn't even know any other reality existed. Then one day, it suddenly ended.

I got my first bad review.

It's hard to explain exactly how it felt to see someone giving my work two stars . . . but I liken it to being punched in the stomach, then the face, then the stomach again. I entered the early stages of what I like to call "critique grief." The first is, obviously, denial. I read her review and then read it again. Turns out, no matter how many times I read it, she still thought my work was "trite" and "ridiculous." Next up? In real-life grief stages it would be anger, but for *critique grief*, at least for me, believing the bad stuff was so much easier than believing the good. Nah, no anger for me—I went right to bargaining. The first idea in my people-pleasing brain was to comment and try to get her to understand my intentions with the work. Better yet, maybe I could find a way to befriend her! Because surely if we became social media acquaintances, and then social media besties, *then* she would know me and therefore better understand my writing. Surely then she wouldn't have disliked it quite so much.

I felt sick to my stomach as I slipped into the last stage of critique grief: acceptance. I decided if this unknown woman was right, maybe everyone else was too easy on my book because it was a debut novel. Maybe *this one person* was a better judge and I was, in fact, a terrible writer.

I was spiraling.

In the midst of it, I heard that little voice in my head that helps me out in times of crazy. No, not God or Jiminy Cricket or even my inner self. The voice in my head is from my therapist, Denise. God bless her.

Years ago Denise told a younger, much more anxiety-ridden me: "Someone else's opinion of you is none of your business."

Let me say that again for the people in the cheap seats.

SOMEONE ELSE'S OPINION OF ME IS NONE OF MY BUSINESS.

Someone else's opinion of *you* is none of *your* business. Those words are so powerful for anyone who tends to hold other people's opinions ahead of their own; and they are never more profound than when we're creating something. Maybe it's a book, a blog, a company, a piece of art, or your fashion sense. When you're creating something from your heart, you do it because you can't *not* do it. You produce it because you believe your creation deserves to be out in the world. You work and work and then you close your eyes and cross your fingers and hope it finds recognition. But here's the thing about that magical, mystical thing you're making: You create because you have a God-given ability to do so. You create as a gift to yourself and to the higher power who blessed you with those abilities. But you can't *make* people like or understand it.

You have to be willing to put it out there even if they don't like it. Even if they hate it. Even if they give it two stars or none at all. You have to understand that every person on earth has an opinion, and their opinion—even if they're the most widely recognized expert on the subject—only has bearing on *your* work if you let it. A mean review cannot make me a bad writer. Can I write terribly?

Oh *heck* yes!

The first (second and third) draft of everything I write is basically garbage. If I refuse to take constructive criticism from an editor I trust, if I don't push myself to grow as a writer, if I regurgitate the same story over and over, or worse, if I try to impersonate someone else's style—then yes, there's a good chance my work is going to suck. But deciding that something is bad simply because other people don't like or understand it is not a theory I can co-sign.

Art and creativity are so subjective, and *dang it*, it's hard to find the courage and drive to complete anything. So, sister, if you're going to work that hard on a project, do you really want to allow it to be blown apart by something as flimsy as an opinion?

As an artist or a creator, you have to decide. You have to choose a path or live the rest of your life slowly killing your ability to do great work for fear of what others will think. You have to decide that you care more about creating your magic and pushing it out into the world than you do about how it will be received.

This task is much easier said than done.

As I sit writing this chapter in my favorite local coffee shop, I've checked my other browser approximately thirty times. This morning I posted an article on a website I've contributed to for years. But today I decided to talk about something a tad bit controversial—at least, it's outside of the kind of post I'm typically known for there. And so now I'm wondering, *Will anyone get it? Will it find a home and an audience?* Or worse yet, *Will it make anyone mad?*

Even after years of putting myself out there, I still get caught up in the lie that I might be a terrible writer or that I should create *or not* based on whether I have an audience for it. I start to believe that I need public opinion to validate my desire to make something, when the truth is, I should embrace my creativity because it's a God-given ability. Any time I try something new, I will have to fight off the desire to confirm that it will be loved in order to keep going. Since I anticipate being creative and trying new things for as long as I'm living, that could mean decades of occasionally being trapped by unhelpful anxieties.

What a waste of energy.

Would I rather bottle up my creative thoughts and ideas? No. I hope they find a home . . . even if they only resonate with a handful of people. So then I have to ask myself if I would be willing to risk a negative response if my work resonated positively with others? What if only one person gets it, but everyone else hates it? What if nobody loves it at all?

Would it be worth it even then?

Yes.

My answer is yes. I would rather put my work out there no matter what the response will be. I would rather create in celebration of the fact that I have the ability to do so.

For me the answer is to create. That is *always* the answer. My personal form of creation is writing—especially writing words I hope other people will enjoy.

So I have two choices: I can write down words and send them out into the world and hope they find a home. Or I can hide my light under a bushel because I'm too afraid someone won't like the glare.

I choose this.

I choose to sit in coffee shops and on airplanes and at my kitchen counter writing. I choose to squeeze in minutes between soccer practice or before sunrise or long after everyone else in the house is asleep to type and type and type until I stream enough sentences together to make a book.

I have no idea if you'll love it or hate it.

Obviously, I hope you dig the heck out of it and buy a hundred copies for all of your friends. But even if you don't, I'll still be here.

I started at this desk alone, without an audience to read my work. I'll stay here as long as I've got words jumbling around in my head, whether or not there's anyone to receive them.

———

When I was a little girl I spent every Sunday (and most other days) at the small First Assembly of God church where my daddy was the pastor. Our song service included Mama on the piano and a handful of tambourines sprinkled throughout the room. We were simultaneously off-key and in three-part harmony in a way only a small country church can pull off.

As I got older I experienced the sedate musicality of a large Presbyterian congregation, the joy of an inner-city gospel choir, and the theatrics of a megachurch. I've been to tiny prayer meetings in Ethiopia where I couldn't understand a single word but *felt* every one of them. I've spent hours upon hours of my life singing and clapping in church, and this is what I've come to discover:

Writing—for me—is its own kind of worship.

The definition of *worship* is "the feeling of expression or reverence for a deity." Creating is the greatest expression of reverence I can think of because I recognize that the desire to *make something* is a gift from God. The freedom to carve out the time and have a safe place to create that art is a blessing of the highest level in a world where so many people are unable to have either. Every time I indulge in the art of creation without worrying about what the public will think of it is craft in its purest form—and craft can be any old thing at all. For me it's writing. For you it might be painting, making quilts, or taking a Thursday-night ballet class. Whether or not something is good or worthy is up for interpretation, and if you're unconcerned about other people's interpretations, then everything you make is *fantastic*.

I hope you'll remember this in your own life, and I hope you'll create for *yourself. Do it* in celebration of your ability to do so, regardless of what anyone else thinks.

THINGS THAT HELPED ME . . .

1. *I stopped reading reviews.* This is a big deal, you guys. I have no idea what you think of anything I've written since that bad review on *Party Girl* so many years ago. Maybe you love

my books, maybe you use them for kindling . . . either way, it doesn't affect my desire to keep writing more. Everyone gets reviewed, even if you're just asking for the opinion of your judgmental sister and being torn apart by her response. Do something daring this year and stop "reading" your version of reviews.

2. *I write for myself.* I write fiction about girls falling in love in Los Angeles. I write cookbooks about cheese-based dips. Now here I am writing a nonfiction book about the struggles and triumphs in my life. This makes no earthly sense. Authors write in one or two genres, and they build up clout in a handful of areas. Here's the bottom line: writing is my art, my creative outlet. It is literally my lifelong dream come true, and therefore, I hold it sacred. It never has been, and never will be, my job. I don't need it to make money to be valuable. This is an important distinction for me because I never want the creative choices I'm making to be based on money or business rather than whatever is on my heart and in my head. If you have it within your power to keep a piece of your creativity just for yourself, it is truly a gift.

3. *I indulge in silliness.* I color with my boys. I draw on the ground with sidewalk chalk. I watch YouTube videos about how to do shimmery, smoky eyes and try to replicate it even if I have nowhere to go. I reach for silly, creative endeavors that serve no real purpose other than joy.

CHAPTER 15

The lie:

I WILL NEVER GET PAST THIS

Since I'm talking about the hard things I've battled and conquered in the stretch of my life, I would be remiss to leave out the one thing I didn't think I could overcome. Anyone who's ever been through something truly traumatic, regardless of how the repercussions have manifested, deserves to hear that they're not alone.

There are many types of trauma—big, small, childhood, adult—but we all belong to a club we never asked to join. We find solidarity in numbers, in hearing other stories . . . and this is mine.

My big brother, Ryan, was funny and unfailingly kind. He had an almost prodigious ability to pick up any instrument and teach himself to play it by ear within the span of a single day. He was handsome. I didn't know it then because I was younger and not inclined to think about it, but when I look back at photos now and see his cocky grin and his startling blue eyes, I realize how good-looking he was. When I was a young girl, he was my best friend and constant playmate. I can still see the two of us vividly in my memory, staying up late in our room playing the alphabet game: "My name is Carla. I'm going to California to sell Crabapples. My name is David. I'm going to Delaware to sell Dogs . . ."

As an adolescent, he was my protector. He taught me how to handle a bully, how to throw a punch, and how to thread a ramen noodle through my nose and out my mouth. He wasn't necessarily better or worse than anyone else's big brother, but he was mine and I loved him. He was my big brother until I was about twelve years old, when his mental illness took over.

He took his own life before I turned fifteen.

I know the reality of that sentence is heavy. But here I am admitting the worst of the worst—the ugly truth of my brother's disease and the destruction of the family it left behind.

I don't know any way to the other side of this conversation without trudging through it. I don't know any other way to offer solidarity to others who've gone through their own trauma without describing my own. Not many people want to share that a member of their family was borderline schizophrenic. Not many people want to tell you that their sibling was severely depressed and obsessive compulsive, going through multiple doctors and countless mood-stabilizing medications before he was even old enough to get a learner's permit.

Very few people would tell you that in his worst moment, my big brother got access to a handgun and left the discovery of his body to me.

I don't want to talk about the nightmares that came afterward, or the crippling fear that I experienced. For years afterward, I assumed every sleeping person, sitting person, unmoving person I encountered must be dead too. I don't want to talk about how when some well-meaning family members came to clean up his room, they covered the bloody wall with the only paint we had on hand that day. I don't want to tell you that because of that, seeing silver spray paint still makes me sick to my stomach. I don't want to tell you about the horrific images that are seared into my brain, or the guilt I carry to this day because I was too afraid to sit with his body until the paramedics arrived. I don't want to talk about all of the therapy I had to sit through as a scared fourteen-year-old, or as an angry seventeen-year-old, or as an adult grappling with the idea that I needed to make up the difference for his loss. I don't want to tell you about how many times I have obsessively planned out the funeral of my husband or my children as a sick coping mechanism for my fear that something could happen to them too.

I don't want to tell you about any of these hidden, ugly, dark truths . . . but I will. I will tell you about my trauma in some of its gruesome detail because I want you to know that there was a time when I didn't think I could wade through it. There was a time when even with my future stretched out in front of me, all I could see was blood and fear and loss.

But I am still here.

And so are you.

I am still here because I refuse to let anything or anyone decide what I get to have. I am still here because I refuse to let my trauma have the last word. I am still here because I will not let a nightmare have more power than my dreams. I am still here because I didn't allow the hard time to make me weak; I willed it to make me strong.

Recently I was watching Tony Robbins's documentary *I'm Not*

Your Guru, and he said, "If you're going to blame your hard times for all the things that are wrong in your life, you better also blame them for the good stuff too!" I was stunned to have something tangible to explain the way I have felt about my brother's death. You're not supposed to acknowledge the good things that come out of trauma . . . there's something perverse and unhealthy about it. It seems wrong to look for any silver lining, because that means appreciating something terrible that happened to you. But I recognize now that if you don't look for the good that came out of what you've lived through, it's all wasted.

I would give nearly anything to have my brother here with us—to know him whole and healthy. To lose him was so devastating I could easily have allowed it to destroy me. What happened to my nerves, my sleep, my sense of safety, and worse, my sense of trust because of having seen him that way, might have totally crippled me. Instead, I flipped the narrative inside my mind. Even as a teenager I used to think, *You can do this, Rachel. You can do anything. Think of what you've lived through already!*

When I moved to Los Angeles at seventeen, where I didn't know anyone or anything and could barely afford to survive, I refused to give in to fear. Sleeping in a crappy apartment, living off food from the ninety-nine-cent store, and barely making rent weren't ever truly scary. I'd lived through real terror, and I knew the difference.

When I was in my fifty-first hour of labor with my first baby and I was weak with exhaustion, my internal monologue reminded me how strong I was. *You were forged in a fire worse than this . . . You've stood with death, and you are certainly strong enough to help bring this life into being!* I've run marathons. I've built companies. I've pushed myself and my career to places further than other people might have believed possible. And the entire time I knew I was capable of it because I knew I'd already lived through worse. Maybe if you haven't lived through anything hard, you find the idea obtuse or even Machiavellian.

But what is the alternative? We live through something crappy, and that's it? We're done for? We allow all the hard, ugliest parts of our lives to color everything else?

You cannot ignore your pain. You cannot ever leave it behind completely. The only thing you can do is find a way to embrace the good that came out of it—even if it takes you years to discover what that is.

Losing my brother was the worst thing that's ever happened to me in my life . . . but it does not *define* my life. You can live through something that rocks your world off its axis. You can survive losing a piece of your heart without losing the core of who you are. More than merely surviving the loss, you can thrive. You can do it because it's what you deserve. More importantly, you can survive the loss because living is the greatest honor you can give to the person you lost . . . even if the person who's gone was your younger, more innocent self.

The path through hardship or extreme trauma is one of the most difficult things a being can encounter. But make no mistake: the only way is to fight *through* it. Pain and trauma are a violent whirlpool, and they will drag you under if you don't battle to stay afloat. There will be times, especially in the beginning, when it will take everything within you to keep your head above those waves.

But you *must* keep your head above the waves. It's so difficult, but you are tough. Even if you don't feel it at the time, the very fact that you're still breathing in and out means you're fighting back against the tide that wants to sweep you away. Don't let it. After a while I promise it will become easier to tread water, and finally you'll learn to swim against the current. The friction you'll face will build your muscles, bones, and sinew—the very fabric of your being will be shaped by this journey. The toughest one you've ever taken, surely . . . but you will become something greater because of it. You have to. Otherwise, what was the point?

I used to naïvely say that "everything happens for a reason." But that was only because I hadn't yet lived through something horrific enough to bring that statement into question. I don't believe everything happens for a specific reason, but I do believe it's possible to find purpose—even in the absence of explanation.

THINGS THAT HELPED ME . . .

1. *Going to therapy.* I know I've already mentioned this, but in this instance, it's worth repeating. I cannot fathom how I would have survived all that I have without the help of a trusted therapist. The process wasn't fun or easy, and I often hated sitting on a couch week after week reliving the trauma; but if I hadn't done that work, it would still be haunting me.

2. *Talking about it.* Not just with a therapist but with at least one other person you trust. When we were first married I sat down one night and told Dave everything about the day Ryan died. Details that had been locked inside my head for six years all fell into the sacred space between us. He didn't try to fix it or organize it or adjust it in any way. He listened, and in doing so, willingly took my pain inside himself and made the load lighter to bear.

3. *Making myself think about it.* Right after Ryan died, I really struggled with nightmares and obsessing over the images in

my head. An extremely wise therapist suggested I set a timer every day for five minutes, then force myself to remember it in detail until the timer went off. I thought he was insane. Turns out, there was something about knowing I would think of it later at an appointed time that allowed my brain the peace of not playing it on a loop. It also meant that I felt in control of my thoughts again. I am so grateful for this wisdom, and I've given it to fellow trauma survivors over and over. I even wrote it into my fictional book *Sweet Girl* as the advice Max gets from her best friend. You really do just write what you know.

CHAPTER 16

The lie:

I CAN'T TELL THE TRUTH

Do I have the courage to tell you this whole story?

That's what I'm asking myself even as I type these words. For days now, in moments when my mind is spinning with all the questions and what-ifs, I've asked myself how I would explain all of this . . . How I *could* tell you this story.

Honestly? I don't want to.

I want to keep it close to my heart, to hide it away in the hopes that it will hurt me less if it stays hidden. But then I understand that when things are hidden, we give power to the fear, the negativity, the lies. I don't want to allow that to happen. I want so badly to be honest about our experience—mostly because I didn't know this experience was even a possibility and because I wish I had truly understood.

Would it have changed our choices?

I'm not sure. But the hope that by being honest about what's happened to our family we might empower or inform other prospective adoptive families is what has me writing these words down now. I hope I have the courage to include them in this book, because truthfully, after building a career based on total honesty . . . I hesitate telling you this now.

But here it is.

When I was pregnant with our son Ford, we decided that we wanted to adopt a little girl someday. As Christians we are called to care for the orphans, the widows, and the oppressed. These are not just a handful of words from the Bible; they are the tenets of my faith. And so we began to research our options and settled on international adoption. Our reasoning—the irony of which is not lost on me in hindsight—was that we were afraid of involvement from biological parents. We were so naïve about so many things back then, but our fear was that biological parents might come back into the picture and take the baby back. We reasoned that if we were an ocean apart, that scenario would be impossible. Eventually we narrowed our search down to Ethiopia.

I remember feeling so overwhelmed by the paperwork, the blood tests, the home visits. I had no idea we were at the very beginning of a journey that would last nearly half a decade. So without any real perspective, I planned and dreamed and waited for news from our agency that we were slowly inching our way up the list. We were in the Ethiopian program for two years.

Toward the end of the second year we received word that Ethiopia was "pausing" its adoption program, and our agency told us to consider moving to another country's program. I felt frozen about what to do next. Moving to a new country meant starting all over again. New paperwork, new meetings, new waiting lists . . . I believed God had called us to Ethiopia, and I believed if we were faithful he would make a way. We decided to stay in the program. Every month we'd get an email from the agency.

Still no movement.

The government office that handles adoptions is still on hiatus.

No word.

Six months later they closed adoptions to the United States completely.

I felt stunned and unsure. If God had called us here, and if nothing came out of the work and pain and fear, what had been the point? All the dreams I'd had about going to Africa as a family to meet our daughter made me feel foolish in retrospect. For the first time I asked myself questions that would pop up again and again over the next several years: *Should we still try and adopt? Should we just feel content with the incredible blessing we have in our three sons? Should we give up?*

I am not by nature someone who sits long with a problem. I am also not someone who gives up. I started to pray and research and scour the internet for what we should do next.

Maybe we were supposed to do domestic adoption . . . Maybe we'd gone through what we did because we were always meant to adopt our daughter from the States and she wasn't even born yet. That answer felt right, so I researched some more.

The more I looked into what was available, the more I believed we should adopt from foster care. We felt called to Ethiopia because they have an unrelenting orphan crisis, and we thought we could help there in some small way. Foster care was the same for me. There were so many children in Los Angeles County who needed love and care; both were things we could offer in abundance. In LA, you have to commit to doing foster care before you can be entered into the adoption program. At first we were terrified of what this would mean for our family or how it would affect our boys. Then we decided that exposing the kids to this reality and showing them how we could tangibly show up for other families who need us was worth it.

We entered the system for foster-to-adopt.

What we didn't know at the time was how difficult that journey was. We didn't understand that we'd get foster placement with a medically frail baby and that the department would have no knowledge of her extreme medical need. We didn't know that they would call us three days after she arrived and beg us to take her two-year-old sister—going from a family of five to a family of seven in a matter of days. We didn't understand the delicate dance of managing a relationship with biological parents who were, in many ways, children themselves. I personally didn't understand how traumatic it would be for me when the girls eventually transitioned out three months later.

I mourned the loss of the foster girls and tried to wrap my brain around what I now knew about this broken system. I thought we'd have months before we got a call for adoptive placement.

It came thirty-four days later.

I was sitting in my office at work when I received an email from our social worker. The subject line was: *Twins?*

We never anticipated taking twins. We weren't signed up for two babies at all, but apparently agreeing to take on the second girl in our foster care journey had made it possible for us to consider it.

We weren't told much about them. The girls were three days old, they'd been abandoned by their mother at the hospital . . . and we had thirty minutes to decide. We sat on the phone together and talked through it while freaking out. Newborn twins? Could we do it? Were we ready after so recently experiencing the loss in foster care? We prayed it over, and ultimately we called the social worker and said the biggest yes of our whole lives.

After waiting four years for an adoption call, we barely slept that night. We spent hours coming up with names. We were so excited we couldn't eat the day we went to pick them up. At the hospital I thought I might be sick waiting for them to bring the babies into the room. And then there they were—so precious and tiny and beautiful I felt like the luckiest person in the whole world because they were ours. Certainly I knew that in foster-to-adopt there would be hurdles and roadblocks, but the story we were told about them led us to believe that reunification was a slim possibility. We took them home and didn't sleep for days because, well, newborn twins. But we didn't even care. It was one of the happiest times of my life.

Four days later, at ten o'clock at night, the police rang our doorbell.

What a harsh and shocking sound. I was so surprised when I heard the doorbell that night that I wondered if a package was being delivered—that's how outside the realm of possibility this was for us. The doorbell rang in the middle of the night and my first thought was, *Is that the almond butter I ordered?*

I think that memory is the hardest for me; I mark it as the last moment I still held on to a naïveté about how things really functioned in the world we were now a part of.

It wasn't FedEx.

It was two police officers, informing us that someone had made an anonymous call to the child abuse hotline about our family for our previous foster care placement.

I stood on my front porch wearing boxer shorts with little hearts on them. My mind was foggy from sleep deprivation, and

I tried so hard to understand the words that were coming out of their mouths.

Over the next few days I would learn just how common this practice is in the foster care system. Because the child abuse hotline is anonymous, anyone can do it. Anyone can say whatever they want. They can do it for spite, to harm your family, to draw attention away from themselves, or a million other reasons I'd prefer not to think about anymore. I obsessed over them for days, and the obsessing did nothing. No matter what we said or did, we could not escape it. The result of a phone call like that is an intense investigation.

Now, let me pause here and say that an investigation is necessary. *Of course it is.* Child abuse is a horrendous, deplorable crime, and if the system doesn't investigate it, how will they protect the children in foster care? I understand this on an intellectual level. On another level, I had to sit in my living room and listen to someone from the Department of Child and Family Services (DCFS) ask my sons questions about whether or not "Mommy and Daddy ever hit each other when they got really, really mad." Or if someone ever "touched them underneath their underwear."

I tried so hard to be strong for my boys in those moments. I tried to keep a smile on my face while holding an eight-day-old baby and telling them, "It's okay, buddy, just answer them honestly."

When the boys left the room, I sobbed quietly while signing documents that gave the DCFS office the right to pull the boys' medical records, to review their school documents, and to ask them further questions.

The whole time the litany that kept playing on repeat in my mind was, *I am the one who pushed us to do foster care. I exposed my family to this system.* I worked so hard to make sure my children would never experience the trauma I'd experienced as a girl, yet I'd unwittingly called it down on our family.

I had no idea.

I was so extremely naïve about what could happen to us. I assumed that the worst thing we'd manage would be the trauma the children in foster care had been exposed to . . . It never occurred to me we'd be attacked simply by virtue of being involved in that world. And I knew—*we knew*—we were completely innocent of this suspicion, but ultimately our record will show "inconclusive." Not "innocent," because how can they clearly say we are innocent when they are working with accusations and the child in question is too young to speak? This isn't a system where you are innocent until proven guilty. This is a system where you are guilty until deemed *inconclusive.*

During this time so many people on social media asked me why I was suddenly so skinny . . . They wanted to know which diet I was doing so they could try it too. It was because for weeks we had investigators from Child Protective Services sitting in our living room questioning our character, asking us if we'd ever gotten so upset we'd shaken a baby.

But are you sure, Mrs. Hollis? Maybe when you were really overwhelmed?

I barely ate. I couldn't sleep without taking medication to help me.

All of this happened while we had newborn twins.

And then, in the midst of this nightmare of pain and confusion, we found out that the girls weren't really available for adoption. Their biological father wanted them. Turns out, *he'd always wanted them* and we'd never been told. They were *never* actually up for adoption. They were definitively in foster care and had only needed placement until his court date. The justification for the omission of this information from the social worker when we found out was, "Well, they could be up for adoption at some point if he steps out of line."

The reasoning was disgusting, frankly—but honestly, I can't even blame her. I can't fathom how many children's files come across her desk in a given week. I can't even imagine how many kids she's desperately trying to find a bed for. So if she has new-born twins popping up in foster care and she can't find a home for them (something we later found out had happened), well then, do you reach out to a good family who's licensed to take two at once? Do you mention that they're abandoned but leave out details about other biological family because the alternative is that they don't have anywhere to go? Do you take advantage of a family who is strong and capable because you have three-day-old babies who are vulnerable?

Probably. And that's exactly what happened to us.

I'm trying to think of how to explain the way this knowledge hit me, and I just don't have the words.

We got a call for the twins after four years of waiting to adopt. That call felt like the answer to years of prayer. But soon we were living a nightmare.

When they left, I felt cheated. I felt tricked. I felt devastated to the marrow of my bones. But it feels important to tell you that it was ultimately our decision to let them go. Honesty was not always offered to us during this process, which is why it feels so important for me to speak it here: We could have agreed to keep the twins. We could have signed on for nine months or twelve months or eighteen months of foster care with the court-ordered two-hour visits, three times each week with the biological father, in the hopes that *maybe* it would turn into adoption.

We couldn't do it.

Or, I suppose that's not right. We *could* have done it . . . but my heart was shredded and my faith in the system was gone.

I fought with myself. Every day for weeks I fought with myself and tried to think of solutions. *Maybe if we . . . But what if they . . . Maybe the dad would . . .*

I fought with God too.

Him most of all.

What was all this for? Why were we here? What did we do to deserve any of this? What about the girls? The ones I named and walked the room with for hours as they worked drugs from their system? What about Atticus, with her big, bright eyes? What about Elliott, who was smaller and needed extra cuddles? *What will become of her, Lord?*

I cried.

I cried so much my eyes were swollen all the time. I cried when I held the girls. I cried when I hesitated to hold the girls, when I warned myself not to keep attaching to someone I would not get to hold on to. I cried when I saw other new mamas on Instagram . . . A few weeks before I had thought we were all part of a tribe.

After all this happened, Dave and I felt so alone. Who could possibly understand what we'd gone through? Would people even believe us when we told them we were being accused of something so far beyond reality for our family we didn't even know it existed? Would anyone understand what it feels like to know that some anonymous person was so vindictive they'd pull us into this horrific scenario just for spite? Will the people who read this story shake their heads and say, "Well, that's what you get for going through foster care"?

It's a mess. It's all a big, hard mess—and it wasn't even finished. Even after the twins left, we still had to endure the investigation—because it wasn't just about judging us for children in the system; it was judging if we were suitable to care for *all children,* including our own. Since we'd opened our home, our medical paperwork, our school files, access to friends and colleagues who can vouch for us as parents—no evidence existed to validate the phony claim.

Nonetheless, it was terrifying. It was ugly and traumatic, as if we were being abused. We had been attacked, and for weeks and weeks we lived in a state of shock.

I've been afraid to write this story. I hesitate to tell you our particular reality because I still believe that the children in foster care deserve advocates. But I think if we had been better prepared for the realities—that abuse allegations are an extremely common occurrence; that you might get inaccurate or misleading information about the children; that regardless of your best intentions, your heart might be broken in ways you can't fathom. I think if we had been informed, I wouldn't feel so hurt now.

Maybe I could have better prepared myself. Maybe that's wishful thinking. *Maybe* is the word that plagued me all day long. In the midst of all of the pain and questioning and wondering, we had something big to decide: Would we continue to try and adopt?

My gut instinct said *absolutely not.*

International adoption and foster-to-adopt weren't areas we felt comfortable exploring anymore, which left us with independent adoption. Dave had preferred this option from the beginning, but I felt like there was a greater need in international or foster care. But now he was asking me to consider it again, and I needed to make a decision quickly.

One of the hardest parts about adoption is how long it takes. So even if I wasn't sure about moving forward, I knew that in order to secure any chance for the future, we'd need to start a new path as soon as possible. Home visits, blood work, applications, hundreds of pages to fill out . . . It takes a while, and unfortunately, none of it is transferable, so we had to start from scratch. Also, we knew nothing about this world or how to even go about it. Did we go through a domestic agency? Should we get an attorney? It all felt so daunting, especially after what we'd just gone through.

I cannot tell you how incredible my husband was during this time period. If you ask most adoptive couples, they'll tell you that the wife originally came up with the idea. Men statistically struggle with the concept of adoption at first. Certainly there are exceptions to the rule, but most of the time women are the ones who push for it. I was the one who pushed for international adoption, and later, I was the one who urged him to consider foster-to-adopt. Now I was wrung out and incapable of feeling hopeful, but Dave encouraged me to reconsider. I'll remember that conversation for the rest of my life . . . I sobbed in the backyard where the kids couldn't hear us, while he fought for our dream of having a daughter.

"Yes, it's hard! But our dream didn't go away because it *got hard*, Rachel. We're going to have a daughter even if it takes longer . . . The time will pass anyway. We can't give up!"

It was Dave who did the research on an adoption attorney. It was Dave who called friends and colleagues and doctors' offices to get referrals on where we should go. It was Dave who sat on the floor while I typed the first draft of this chapter. He had paperwork spread out in every direction on the first day of his holiday break while he uploaded document after document to our new adoption agency.

The independent adoption process felt more daunting to me than anything we'd done before. In that process a birth mom chooses you to be the parents of her child—which means being in competition with thousands of couples all over the country. It also meant that whenever a mother came up who had criteria that matched with ours, I would get a call from our attorney, who then asked us to call a stranger and have the most surreal conversations. This happened three times in the first two months. I think the optimistic view should have been that we had three opportunities in such a short time, but the truth—because I'm trying to be totally honest with you—is that those experiences felt brutal. I know I shouldn't have gotten my hopes up, but it was impossible not to get excited when I spoke to a birth mom. I'd hear about her due date and listen to her story and start to think, *Oh my gosh, what if this is the one? What if we have a baby in April?*

When we weren't the family she chose, I'd feel foolish for being hopeful. I'd wonder if this was all a big waste of time or a painful experiment that led nowhere. Were we ever going to have a daughter? *Should we still even want one?* I'd wonder. And my sadness . . . was it disrespectful to be sad when I had three beautiful boys and other families didn't have any? I would sit in our bathroom and cry while my mind spun with all of these questions. I never truly found answers.

What I did cling to was faith. Sometimes that faith was tenuous, as though I could barely hang on to it. But it was still there—that small voice that urged me to keep trying. *Just one more step*, God would whisper. "Tomorrow will be better," Dave would tell me. *Someday I'll hold my daughter in my arms and I'll understand why I waited for her,* I reminded myself over and over again.

During those months that we waited, I walked in faith. My steps weren't bold or filled with the bravado I'd had at the beginning of the journey nearly five years before. My faith walk became cautious and unsure. I blindly stumbled my way down a path I could not see. I chose to move forward because, while I knew I would find pain, I also knew I would draw strength. I could look at the six months prior or five years in total and choose to be angry. Or I could look at the whole long journey and recognize all that we'd been given.

We knew about the orphan crises, both domestic and international. We donated time and money and prayers and resources to helping with something that wasn't even on our radar before. That is why I kept walking in faith.

We got to know and love four little girls, and even if we never see them again, our lives are better because we were connected for a time. That is why I kept walking in faith.

We built a stronger marriage. If you go through that much together, it will either make you stronger or break you apart. Dave and I sat in a foxhole of paperwork and interviews and blood tests and invasive questions. Later, we learned how to care for toddlers with severe trauma and newborn twins who screamed all night. We have laughed and cried and come out the other side braver, bolder, and more connected. That is why I kept walking in faith.

I can think of so many good things that came out of all that happened, which gives me the courage to take another step. It's why I kept calling birth moms even if it meant being disappointed when it didn't work out. It's why I kept praying for our daughter, not knowing who she was or how long it would take us to meet her.

It's why I'll stay hopeful even when I'm feeling weary. It's why I'll keep telling our story even when it's painful to talk about. Because at the end of all of this, I don't want you to see someone who went through a long, intense process to adopt a little girl. I want you to see someone who kept showing up again and again, even when it was tearing her apart. I want you to see someone who kept walking in faith because she understood that God's plan for her life was magnificent—even if it was never easy. And even if it wasn't easy, she was bold and courageous and honest even when the truth was hard to share.

THINGS THAT HELPED ME . . .

1. *Taking the plunge.* Finding the courage to be honest about who you are or what you're going through is like throwing yourself into the deep end of the pool and fighting to swim once you hit the cold water. It won't necessarily be pleasant, but once you're in, it's done. The longer you live in a state of honesty, the easier it becomes to simply exist there all the time.

2. *Seeking out other truth tellers.* Surround yourself with people who've also gone through the hardship of being honest about their feelings. They can talk to you about how it felt and how they found the courage. They can also stand as an example of someone who admitted their hardship and lived to tell about it.

3. *Researching stories similar to my own.* If we had done more advance research into foster care in LA, what happened wouldn't have been so shocking to us. Having walked through it now, and knowing more people who have too, makes us realize how common our experience was. During the process we felt so alone, and seeking out a community who understood our path would have helped so much.

CHAPTER 17

The Lie:

I AM DEFINED BY MY WEIGHT

When people talk about divorce, they use words like *irreconcilable* or *messy*. But those words are too light—too easy for the destruction of a family. Divorce is a book falling onto a house made of Legos. It's a cannonball shot over the bow that crashes through the deck and sinks the other ship. Divorce is destruction that starts at the top and breaks everything apart on the way down. So, no. *Messy* isn't the right adjective.

Horrible, ugly, hateful, annihilating—these are closer.

When I was sixteen, my parents were in the middle of a horrible, ugly, hateful, annihilating divorce that had been on again, off again since I was nine years old.

During this season—the final death throes of their relationship—I had just received my driver's license and a hand-me-down car.

It was a 1989 Suzuki Samurai, and it was also a stick shift—something I had no earthly clue how to operate. It sat for weeks in the driveway collecting dust—an eyesore of a reminder that it wasn't being used and that I wasn't capable of operating it.

I hinted to my older sister, to her boyfriend, and to my mother, hoping that someone would take me out on a weekend or an afternoon and explain the intricacies of operating a clutch. If I knew how to drive that car, I could get myself to school. If I knew how to drive that car, I could get a job and start saving money. So many possibilities existed on the other side of that manual transmission.

One day, out of nowhere, my father decided he would be the one to teach me how. And even then, amid the excitement of wanting to know how to drive myself around, I knew this was a catastrophically bad idea.

Daddy had a hair-trigger temper. It was an ever-present part of my life growing up, but during this time period, it was so much worse. We were only a little over a year and a half removed from the death of my big brother, Ryan.

In retrospect I can see that my father was struggling for normalcy, that he was trying to parent the only child he had remaining at home. He was also trying to teach me to drive stick shift in my brother's car—the hand-me-down made possible because Ryan didn't need it any longer.

What must that have felt like for him—or for any of them who had hesitated to take me out driving in Ryan's car? Had Daddy drawn the proverbial short straw? Was he the only one strong enough to move past the pain and do what needed to be done? Perhaps another person would have battled their emotions in a different way. Perhaps my mother would have cried or my sister would have lashed out, but my father . . . his strong emotions tended to bubble in only one direction: straight to the boiling point.

I didn't understand any of my pain or trauma at the time. Likewise, I was sixteen and couldn't fathom why my father was so angry. We'd driven to the outskirts of town where I could practice without other cars around. I can still see us on that abandoned country road as he screamed commands into the air between us: "Clutch! Shift! Gas! How many times are you going to stall out before you get this right?"

The more he screamed, the more I stalled. The more I stalled, the more I cried. The more I cried, the angrier he became.

I have no idea if that episode lasted for ten minutes or an hour. I only know that I retreated further and further inside myself until I was shaking. He finally demanded to drive.

We rode home in tense silence.

As an adult I can understand now how hard he battled his temper with us kids and how upsetting it was for him to lose it. An executive, a pastor, and later a PhD, he was utterly competent out in the world but often at a loss at home. I can see that now. As a child I was blind to it all. I spent most of my life in fear of upsetting him. In a situation like this, where I had well and truly failed and he was so, so angry, I wished—not for the first time—that I was the child he'd lost.

He dropped me off at home, and I found myself in an empty house scared and confused and sick to my stomach. Then I walked to the kitchen.

I come from a long line of emotional eaters, so my first thought was that something in that kitchen would surely make me feel better. I found an unopened box of Oreos and I pulled out two. They tasted so good I had another.

I remember sliding down to the floor alongside the cabinets

with the box in my hand. I'd been here plenty of times before. Food is an easy companion. Food has never let me down. Only this time, something shifted. With each cookie I ate, I cried harder. Then I ate more. At some point, the noise in my head shifted. It stopped being about my dad and why he was so angry. I thought about myself and all the ways and reasons that I was wrong. *Good*, I thought, *eat them all. Eat every last cookie. Eat everything in this room. Eat until you're ugly and worthless and the outside finally matches the inside.*

I sat on that floor and I cried and ate until I was sick.

That was the first time I remember punishing myself with food, but it wouldn't be the last.

My issues with my body—the way I saw it and, subsequently, *myself* by association—didn't start that day, but I do think they took a flying leap from something that may have affected me peripherally to something that became front and center in my life. My weight was no longer just a part of me like hair or teeth; now it was something that *defined* me. It was a testament to all the ways I was wrong.

Later on that same year, I got mono. I wish I could tell you that it was because I had an intense make-out session with a teenage vampire, but in fact, I caught it from some water fountain outside honors chem. I was bedridden for a week and could barely swallow, let alone eat anything.

When I emerged from the haze of sickness I'd lost a massive amount of weight. I was so very tiny. I couldn't stop staring at myself in the mirror. I wanted to buy new jeans in this new size. I was positive that my life was now going to be everything I'd ever hoped for. I would be popular, I would go to parties, I would attract the attention of Edward Cullen . . . I mean, as a size two, *anything* is possible and everything is likely. I vowed on my soul that I would not gain a single pound back.

But I was hungry. I was so stinking hungry all the time. I know they say nothing tastes as good as skinny feels, but I assume that's because they've never had Nachos BellGrande. I gained the weight back and then some.

When I moved to Los Angeles at age seventeen, I was hyper-aware of how out of place I was as a size ten, and I vowed that geography was really the only thing that had held me back. I was ready to get a gym membership, run a marathon, and eat only salads from there on out—none of which happened. A lifetime of stress eating meant that I gained even more weight after my move.

I decided to try diet pills.

I don't even know what brand they were or where we got them, but for a couple of months, my roommate and I lived off of diet pills and SlimFast shakes. It totally worked. I trimmed down and loved everything about my new, smaller body. Sure, I was hungry all the time and I felt jittery nonstop, but I looked awesome in my jeans.

I expected that life would pick right up and be easy before long, and my dreams would soon manifest and become true. I noticed that more men were checking me out, to the point that the attention was starting to really bother me. Anywhere we went I could feel their eyes staring at me. I expected guys to charge the table anytime we went for dinner. I gave dirty looks to any male within a ten-foot radius. I was not totally sane, but I also wasn't self-aware enough to realize it.

One day I got home from work early, and I happened to look out the apartment window. Across the way I saw two iguanas sunning themselves in the window of someone else's condo. Two iguanas the length of my femur just hanging out in the kitchen window. One of them turned his head slightly, caught my eye, and stared me down. You're going to think I'm making this up, but I swear on my life I thought that lizard was looking into my soul. I was entranced; I couldn't stop staring. I watched those things for what felt like hours, and I became certain that if I didn't keep staring back into his eyes (across a hundred feet of space), something bad would happen. At one point I remember thinking, *When was the last time I saw a human being? Are these iguanas and I the only creatures left on earth?!* My roommate found me like this later that afternoon. When I tried to explain to her what I was feeling—as rationally as I could for someone who had just stared down lizards for hours—she asked, "Do you think it could be the diet pills?"

Well, *now . . .*

I was so grateful to discover that there were more beings on earth than just me and the lizards who'd survived the apocalypse. I ran and grabbed the bottle and read the label for the first time. *May cause extreme paranoia* was side effect número uno. Blessed assurance!

I stopped taking the pills and started eating solid foods again, and just like every other time, the weight piled back on.

I wish I could tell you that extreme paranoia/lizard Armageddon would have been the end of my career in weight obsession or yo-yo dieting, but I can't. I tried all sorts of crazy things. Susan Powter, Suzanne Somers, Atkins, Lean Cuisine, juice cleanses, master cleanses . . . the list goes on. And every single time I would start on a diet and inevitably slip up. One "mistake" (like having a piece of cake at a birthday party) would signal total annihilation to my brain. One piece of cake meant I might as well eat the *entire* cake, plus the chips and the dip and pizza and anything else I could get my hands on. I'd restart that same hateful binge session I'd learned at sixteen in the kitchen with the Oreos.

I had identified at a very early age that women who were thin were beautiful. Thin women would fall in love and have handsome husbands. They would also have career success, make good mothers, have all the best clothes. I don't know that I ever said those words aloud, but I absolutely believed them.

Sixteen years later, this isn't a truth I like to admit. I don't like to talk about my messy childhood or my negative self-talk or the ridiculous lies I used to believe. I don't like to focus on the things I got wrong, but they're like that little crack in the side of a teacup, an imperfection you only see when you hold it up to the light. The imperfections cover the surface of my life; they help tell my story. For good or bad or worse, they're part of me.

Later on when I went through my first pregnancy and subsequent weight gain, this struggle became so much worse. I wanted so badly to be like celebrities I saw in magazines who had a baby and then left the hospital in pre-pregnancy jeans. I held on to those twenty-plus pounds of baby weight for a year, and the second I started to make headway on them, I got pregnant again. I wondered if I would ever get out from under the pounds.

I think this is the part in the typical inspirational and motivational book where the author would tell you that a journey of self-discovery and a lot of therapy helped her learn that weight did not define her. This is where I should tell you that I am worthy and loved as I am. This is absolutely true, but that's not where I'm headed with this chapter. That isn't the kind of book I want to write. Here's what I can tell you truthfully about diet and exercise and weight and what it means in my life.

Who you are today is incredible. You have so many wonderful qualities to offer the world, and they are uniquely yours. I believe your Creator delights in the intricacies of you, and he is filled with joy when you live out your potential.

I also believe that humans were not made to be out of shape and severely overweight. I think we function better mentally, emotionally, and physically when we take care of our bodies with nourishment, water, and exercise. The lie I used to believe was that my weight would define me, that it would speak volumes about who I was as a person. Today I believe it's not your weight that defines you, but the care and consideration you put into your body absolutely does.

Because I work in media and because I've had years of accidentally upsetting people online without ever meaning to do so, I already know that my saying this will annoy some people. I can already imagine the emails I'll get. The list of reasons why you or someone you know is justifiably obese, the trauma you've lived through . . . in some cases, food is your coping mechanism. Or maybe I'll hear the opposite. Maybe you have an eating disorder like anorexia. You're thin but totally unhealthy because your body doesn't get the nutrients it needs. Or maybe you drink every single day because you're a single parent or you're walking through a hard season. All of these things are justifiable, all of these are valid reasons to negate caring for yourself . . . for a time.

Childhood trauma is not a life sentence. Extreme emotional pain doesn't guarantee emotional pain for the rest of your life. I know this is true because I am a living, breathing, flourishing example of someone who chooses to rise above the trauma of her past. The reason I know this is true is because the world is filled with people who have it so much harder than me and so much harder than you, yet they show up for their lives *every single day*.

You can choose whether or not to stay there. You can *choose* to continue to abuse your body because it's all you know. You can *choose* to live in that place because it's the path of least resistance. You can *choose* to settle for a half-lived life because you don't even know there's another way, or perhaps you have no idea how to pull yourself out of it. But please, *please* stop making excuses for the whys. Please stop telling yourself that you deserve this life. Please stop justifying a continued crappy existence simply because that's the way it's always been. Just as you've chosen to stay in this place for so long, you can also choose to get yourself out of it.

You need to be healthy.

You don't need to be thin. You don't need to be a certain size or shape or look good in a bikini. You need to be able to run without feeling like you're going to puke. You need to be able to walk up a flight of stairs without getting winded. You need to drink half your body weight in ounces of water every single day. You need to stretch and get good sleep and stop medicating every ache and pain. You need to stop filling your body with garbage like Diet Coke and fast food and lattes that are a million and a half calories. You need to take in fuel for your body that hasn't been processed and fuel for your mind that is positive and encouraging. You need to get up off the sofa or out of the bed and move around. Get out of the fog that you have been living in and see your life for what it is.

Does your Creator love you as you are? Yes! But he gave you a body with all of its strength, and even its weaknesses, as a gift. It is an offense to your soul to continue to treat yourself so badly.

So no, this isn't the book where I tell you that the answer to your struggle with weight loss is to love and accept yourself as you are. This is the book where I tell you that if you truly want to practice self-love, you'll start with your physical body and do the work to figure out why this is an issue in the first place. Do you think I'd understand my emotional eating if I hadn't done years of therapy to get to the bottom of it? Do you think I'd so easily share the story of that day with the Oreos if I hadn't done everything in my power to step out of that shadow? Do you think I magically figured out how to lose weight after a lifetime of living off cheese and gravy?

No. I had to work.

I had to study and go to therapy. I had to try out different workouts until I found some I love. (For me, it's long-distance running and weight training.) I had to fight the urge to binge when I made slight deviations from healthy eating—and this habit took me *years* to adopt. I had to teach myself new coping mechanisms for stress (sex is a win-win for everyone, for example). I had to figure out how weight loss works and discover that it's actually the simplest thing in the world. A million diets exist based on the idea that if they can confuse you or make you think there is an easy way out, then you'll buy whatever they're selling. The truth is, it's the same now as it always has been.

If the calories you consume in a day are fewer than the calories you burn off in a day, you will lose weight. The end.

Figuring out healthy meals that taste good to you, or workouts to try . . . that might be tougher, but don't let the media fool you into believing that this is complicated. Learning to be healthy when you've never done it before might be hard if you've got a lifetime of habits to break, but the mechanics of it are actually very simple. And the version of you that's healthy and well cared for is worth every minute of that work.

THINGS THAT HELPED ME . . .

1. **Mantras.** In my first fiction book I ever wrote, the main character walks around everywhere she goes reciting a mantra: "I am strong. I am smart. I am courageous." She's nervous and unsure of herself, so she says it over and over all day long. That book

is based on my early days in Los Angeles, and that mantra is based on exactly what I used to say to myself daily. A lifetime of believing that your value—or lack thereof—is determined by your body or your face or your *whatever* means that you've got a lifetime of negative talk in your head playing on repeat. You need to replace that voice with something positive. You need to replace that voice with the opposite truth—the thing you most need to believe. So come up with a mantra and say it to yourself a thousand times a day until it becomes real.

2. ***Editing my media.*** If you're struggling to live up to a certain standard, if it seems as though everywhere you turn you see a gorgeous size-zero model with perfect, glossy hair, and if every time you see this stuff it depresses you or gives you anxiety, then *stop consuming that type of content!* Unfollow the models on Instagram; stop looking at those pages on Facebook. Surround yourself with positive, uplifting role models who focus on being strong and healthy. I'm not saying women who do makeup tutorials or Instagram fitness models are bad (I personally love those chicks!), but there are seasons when following them doesn't make sense. Be smart about it.

3. ***Preparation.*** You have to prepare in advance for anything you want to do well. Period. You want to make sure you get in a workout tomorrow? Then you need to pack your bag today and schedule exercise in your calendar. You want to make sure you reach for healthy snacks instead of your kid's Goldfish crackers? Then you better take some time at the start of the week and meal prep some wholesome snack options. If you wait until the last minute, you are not likely to achieve anything. You want to accomplish a healthier life? Map out how you'll get there.

CHAPTER 18

The lie:

I NEED A DRINK

The first time I ever had a drink of alcohol, I was fifteen years old. It's sounds pretty scandalous, but honestly, it was basically harmless. My big sister Christina let me have a sip of her Midori Sour one night when I was spending the night at her apartment. She made it in a plastic tumbler that came with the purchase of Big Gulps circa 1998—so we were keeping it *way* classy. The drink itself was sweeter than Pixy Stix powder and a shade of neon green that's typically only found in something radioactive. I was excited to try it out because it made me feel mature, but it certainly wasn't a gateway drug to partying at Studio 54.

The second time I had a drink I was seventeen years old. My best friend Kim and I drank half a bottle of cheap tequila between the two of us. It was the color of maple syrup—the kind of high-quality liquor reserved for idiot teenagers and sailors on shore leave. We threw up everything that wasn't permanently attached to our insides, positive we were going to die.

It's a miracle we didn't. It's also a miracle neither of our mamas found out and murdered us in cold blood.

Those first two experiences are pretty solidified in my memory because they were so out of the ordinary. Alcohol was never present in my late teenage years and only made a rare appearance in my early twenties. Oh sure, I had some Boone's Farm just like every other poor, confused, college-age girl . . . but drinking wasn't on my radar. On my wedding day I had a few sips of champagne. On our honeymoon I probably tried some kind of blended drink, but that was really more for the milkshake quality than any medicinal aspects. In fact, I remember going to a dinner party not so long into our marriage and another couple talked about how much wine they consumed. Dave and I drove home talking about it.

"Did you hear how much wine she says she drinks? That's crazy!"

I sat atop my glass house and judged a behavior I couldn't understand.

Then I had kids.

Then I had kids, and wine became my best friend. Cocktails? They were like favorite cousins you only see on the holidays—which is to say, I only really got to enjoy them on special occasions.

Is it funny or depressing to admit that before I had kids, I never really understood why anyone drank? Then suddenly I found myself exhausted, overwhelmed, and on edge. I discovered that I could have a glass of wine that magically muted the edges.

When my older boys were toddlers, drinking became a regular part of my routine. I'd come home from work, change into my pajamas (because bras are the Devil's work), and pour myself a glass of wine while I got dinner ready.

When I was a teenager I watched *Cat on a Hot Tin Roof* and fell in love with Elizabeth Taylor and Paul Newman fighting their way through a Southern plantation. In the film adaptation of that play, Brick has become an alcoholic, and in one scene in particular he's fighting with Big Daddy (played impeccably by Burl Ives) and arguing that he needs a drink. He keeps talking about a click that happens when he drinks enough that makes him feel better.

My teenage self thought Paul Newman was really overselling it, that the description of that "click" was Southern dramatics. But then I started drinking wine in the evening when I got home from work. Without realizing, I counted my way toward that click with every sip of white wine. Between the first swallow and the fifth I'd feel myself start to relax. By the tenth sip I was totally calm, able to parent my children better and more easily.

One glass of wine at night turned into two glasses of wine at night. Two glasses of wine a night turned into a seven-day-a-week habit that increased in quantity on the weekend.

Each morning I would wake up feeling a little queasy or have to take ibuprofen to counteract my headache. Each morning I would chalk it up to hormones or lack of sleep.

I refused to acknowledge my daily hangover for what it was.

At social gatherings or work events I would pound a cocktail or a glass of the signature drink as soon as I got in the room. Being in a crowd made me hyperaware of *getting it right*. I reasoned that if I was more relaxed I'd be better able to carry on more meaningful conversations.

Alcohol gave me courage.

It gave me the courage to parent. It gave me the courage to have conversations with strangers. It gave me the courage to feel sexy. It washed away things like anxiety, fear, frustration, and anger with juicy acidity and a balanced flavor profile.

I'm trying to remember the moment I realized how unhealthy all of this was for me, and I don't have a clear defining instant in my mind. I only recall that one day I suddenly caught myself saying, "I need a glass of wine."

As a writer, I pay a lot of attention to words. In this instance, on this random day, I caught the word *need*.

Need implies that something is essential, necessary. So when had I gone from thinking wine might be a nice addition to my night to believing it was essential for my survival? The idea was terrifying.

Terrifying because I come from a long line of alcoholics and I didn't want to become one myself. I stopped cold turkey. Gave up any kind of alcohol for as long as it took me to realize I didn't actually need it. After about a month without any alcohol, and after discovering that the world would continue to spin on its axis even without it, I felt more in control. I would occasionally have a drink, but truly didn't feel the desire to drink when I was stressed.

And then we had foster kids.

That summer we signed up for the foster-to-adopt system in LA County. We jumped right in. In retrospect we were so euphoric about the time we had with the children, so eager to be helpful. We should have taken a step back before we agreed to anything. We didn't know that at the time, though. We were naïve about all that was coming or how hard it would be, so we said yes and went from three boys to five children in the span of a couple of weeks.

Those days were absolute chaos in the most beautiful way. Dave and I were in straight-up survival mode; our only mission each and every day was to occupy five children between six in the morning and eight o'clock at night. We ran around the yard, jumped on the trampoline, and spent hours and hours swimming in the pool. We navigated severe health issues with the baby and her big sister's trauma. We cleaned up a thousand spills and kissed skinned knees and reminded everyone to be kind at least thirty times a day. And at night, when they were snuggled in their beds? We drank vodka.

Wine? Wine was long gone. Wine wouldn't even touch the level of exhaustion and fear and overwhelm we were feeling. Vodka was my copilot, and I was deeply grateful for its presence in my life. We began to navigate visits with bio parents and medical appointments several times a week. We became entrenched in DCFS and battled against a broken system we were inside of.

How do you keep taking babies to see parents who aren't parenting? How do you give up half a Saturday to wait in a McDonald's playland for addicts who may or may not show up, then hand over an innocent baby and watch them erase whatever progress you've made with their daughter? How do you do all of this *knowing* that they'll be reunited at the end of it all, and there's nothing you can do about it? If you're like me, you find a way. But at night, when no one is looking, you drink, and when it gets really bad, you take a Xanax too.

I look back on that time and feel sad for that version of me. I feel sad for the younger mom who needed her nightly wine and for the woman who was fighting so hard to keep her head above water. On some level I feel like there's a bit of shame as well, because if I can't be strong for myself, I at least want to be strong for my babies. I don't want them to know a version of me that used anything to dull the sharp edges. It makes me hyperaware of that bio mom I met every week at McDonald's, and it makes me consider her addiction in another light. It makes me wonder if maybe some of you reading this now have your own version of this kind of coping too.

Over the last year I've gotten more and more emails from women who are struggling with how much they drink. The drinking isn't enough to be a real problem, they tell me . . . yet. Right now their family and friends think they're just the life of the party, or they don't know how much they're actually consuming. But they worry it's getting worse. They're gaining weight and spending money. Drinking is hard to walk away from because the action is just so easy. One sip, one *click* is all that's standing between them and not screaming at their children. A little bit of alcohol will make the difference between anxiety and ease or frustration and contentment.

For the last few years of my career I've gotten notes from people thanking me for my honesty. I've heard that when I shared my story, other women felt like they're not so alone. Those women who send me notes about their drinking? They've done that for me in return. They've also given me a powerful piece of truth to fight against this lie: my struggle is not unique, and therefore there's nothing wrong with me. If there's nothing wrong with me, I don't have any reason to medicate myself.

Make no mistake: drinking the way I drank is a form of medication. Life felt hard or overwhelming, so I put something into my body to make it feel better. But it was a short-term solution to a problem that was not going away. When the alcohol wore off, my problems were still there. When the vodka ran out, I still had to sit in one of the hardest experiences of my life; I still had to pack up bags for those babies and load them into a car with a social worker to head back to their family.

Drinking can be an attempt to escape, but you cannot escape the realities of your life forever. In the morning they're still there, only now your ability to take them on is diminished by the fact that your "medicine" made you sicker.

In fact, there is only one way to manage the stresses of this life properly, and that is to build up a healthy "immune" system (for lack of a better, cooler description). Stick with me here: I promise these analogies will make sense in a minute.

When you're born, you come screaming into the world without any real protection. Your immune system is basically nonexistent, which is why worriers like me keep their newborns wrapped up like Eskimos even in the middle of summertime. As you get older you'll eventually get sick for the first time, likely because you have an older brother who brings home some kind of virulent flu from preschool with him. Getting sick with something you've never had before can be scary, but it's also entirely necessary to build up your immune system. Once you survive, your body is forever able to battle off that kind of sickness, and it can take on similar types of trouble because it's been through it all before.

Occasionally we'll get an infection that our immune system isn't quite strong enough to manage, so someone prescribes some antibiotics. Back when I was a little girl, they handed out antibiotics for everything! Tonsillitis? Antibiotics. Stub your toe? Antibiotics. Then, at some point in between when I was small and when I had my own children, doctors realized that if you took antibiotics too much, your body would never learn how to fight off anything on its own. Your immune system needed to be put through the test; it needed to get sick and learn what tools were necessary to pull itself out of there.

You see where I'm going, right?

The difficult seasons we walk through are how we learn to build up strength to manage any situation. The strongest people you know? They've probably walked some pretty hard roads and built up the skills necessary to be emotional giants. When they encounter hard things, their seasoned bodies rely on the good antibodies they've built up to handle that sort of scenario. They don't medicate because they're strong enough to manage on their own, and they know that medicating will likely make them weaker.

I had to teach myself better ways to handle stress and painful seasons. I had to teach myself better habits. Having a drink will always be the easiest way out; it requires the least effort but demands the most in retribution. Running, having dinner with my girlfriends, praying, going to therapy, or allowing myself to cry are the best methods I know of for building up the strength necessary to carry on. These habits make me strong enough to handle the hard stuff, meaning I don't reach for the easy way out.

For the longest time I thought I *needed* a drink. Maybe you have no idea what that feels like. Maybe for you the "drink" is prescription pills or food or pornography. Or maybe right now you're reading this and thinking you'd never do anything so dire. I'd ask you, then, to take a good look at your life. I know many women who binge-watch TV or read romance novels obsessively because in those spaces they are closed off from the world; in those spaces they can escape the hard parts of their lives by muting them with distraction. Food, water, shelter, healthy relationships . . . those are things you need. Anything else you insert into that category becomes a dangerous crutch—and you don't need a crutch if you are strong enough to walk on your own.

If you don't feel strong, if as you read these lines you feel weak in your soul . . . I want you to ask yourself if you are pushing to find strength or if you're reaching for a quick fix. Strength is never easy to come by.

It's like building up muscles at the gym. First you have to

break down the weaker parts of yourself before you can build them back up. The process is often painful, and it takes time—often way longer than anyone expects it to. Just like with your immune system, you'll get stronger in one area and then something hard will come along that you've never encountered before. You'll have to learn and grow in a new area, which can feel discouraging if you've already walked through hard seasons in the past. But fighting through those times is how you get tougher; it's how you become the person you were meant to be.

THINGS THAT HELPED ME . . .

1. *Learning about habits.* I read an awesome book last year called *The Power of Habit* by Charles Duhigg. Turns out, so many of our negative behaviors—drinking, smoking, etc.—are long-engrained habits triggered by a specific cue. So for me, I felt stressed out, which cued a bad habit in drinking. By identifying my cue, I could replace it with a better coping mechanism, which for me is time with my girlfriends or a long-distance run.

2. *Acknowledging my reality.* Self-awareness is one of the most important skills to acquire in the world. For months I ignored the negative side effects of drinking, until one day I finally forced myself to acknowledge who I was and what was really going on. It's so easy to ignore weakness like that, particularly if it's wrapped up in self-care or coping; but you're never going to move past a problem if you can't even admit to having it in the first place.

3. *Removing the temptation.* If you're struggling with how much you drink, remove access to alcohol. If you binge-eat

cookies when you get stressed out, don't bring cookies into your home. Obviously real struggles run so much deeper than simply having access, but it's much easier to fall into those temptations if they're sitting right in front of you.

The lie:

THERE'S ONLY ONE
RIGHT WAY TO BE

I grew up in Southern California, but I may as well have been born and raised in West Texas for all the trucks and accents and country music that stretched out along the dusty fields in every direction. Bakersfield is the name of the town that you'd maybe recognize even if you didn't grow up there—but even that is a long shot. I actually came home from the hospital and found my way into adolescence in a tiny town on the outskirts of the outskirts called Weedpatch.

Weedpatch and the surrounding communities were originally established by migrant farmworkers who traveled to California from Oklahoma during the Dust Bowl. Have you read *The Grapes of Wrath*, or more likely, did you ever watch the movie during tenth-grade history class?

Well, those are my people.

My people are from Oklahoma, Arkansas, and Kansas. The generations before them are Irish and Scottish—which is to say, we come from a long history of strong, proud people who are deeply ensconced in their religion and the traditions of their culture. When you add to that the fact that my father was a Pentecostal minister and my grandfather was a Pentecostal minister, it would have been nearly impossible for me to come up into this world without some firm ideas about what it meant to be the *right* way.

The elders in our community didn't point fingers at others as being wrong, but our community only included people who looked and acted and thought the way we did. We were white, low-income, conservative, and extremely churched, with little experience outside a ten-mile circumference of our town.

I didn't know that being *other* was wrong, because I didn't know that *other* existed.

When I was in junior high I went to Disneyland to play fourth-chair clarinet with the symphonic band. It was the first time I'd ever left our hometown without a family member, and the opportunity made me feel positively worldly. They say America is a melting pot, but Disneyland was a salad bowl. No one melted together; they all stood out in glorious diversity. I saw every kind of person. I saw families made up of every ethnicity. There were whole groups of friends waiting in line for the teacups, and not one of them was the same race. Two men were holding hands near the Matterhorn, and my eyes nearly popped out of my skull. Even among the people who looked like me, the individual styles were beyond what I could fathom: goth, preppy, purple hair, piercings, tattoos—I saw everything! It was my first real exposure to people who were different from me, and I hardly knew what to do with the sight other than to stare at them as if they were exhibits in a zoo.

I suppose that there are plenty of young women whose lives are more closed off, more sheltered than my own, but it's shocking for me now to write these things down given the diversity of my grown-up life.

It's been on my mind a lot lately—what I grew up understanding versus what I believe now. It's been on my heart because we're walking through a season of people drawing lines in the sand. As much as I hate to admit it, I understand those lines—I was once drawing them. A schoolyard segregated by everything from race to religion to the cost of the jeans you wore made absolute sense to me because that was all I knew. But you cannot claim a child's ignorance forever. At some point you grow up enough to understand that many people here on earth are different from you; and what you do with that knowledge defines much of your story.

I've built a business based on the idea of community with other women, and it's a digital tapestry of people from all over the world. What I've learned over the years is that regardless of how our looks may differ, we are way more alike than we are different. The mamas who follow me in Dubai have a lot of the same concerns for themselves and their families as the mamas in Manila or Dublin or Mexico City. I believe the Lord gave me this platform to be a good shepherd to this diverse and beautiful flock. I also believe I can't possibly love them well if I first demand that they be like me in order to receive it.

I am a Christian, but I fully love and accept you and want to hang out with you and be friends if you're Christian or Muslim or Jewish or Buddhist or Jedi or love the opposite sex or love the same sex or love Rick Springfield circa 1983. Not only that: I think the ability to seek out community with people who are different from me makes me a stronger, better version of myself. Trying to be in community with people who don't look or vote or believe like you do, though sometimes uncomfortable, will help you stretch and grow into the best version of yourself.

On Saturday mornings I go to hip-hop dance class. And just so we're clear, I don't mean cardio dance at the gym or Zumba—but a real-life, honest to dog, "count of eights as fast as I've ever moved in my whole life" dance class.

And I suck.

I thrust when we're supposed to swerve; I kick when we're supposed to fall back. Imagine your aunt Mildred trying to negotiate the dance floor after one too many Chardonnays during cousin Crystal's third wedding. I'm *that* level of tragic. Because it's so hard to pick up a dance like that when you have no experience, and because I'm surrounded by young, nubile, professional dancers who all seem to have it figured out when I don't, I—more than once—have questioned why I'm there at all.

I'll tell you why I'm there: aside from a deep and abiding love for nineties music, I'd actually like to be a better dancer. I'd actually prefer to go through the hard, confusing process of figuring it out and asking questions and seeking guidance than settling for the cushy comfort zone where life isn't hard, but where I don't grow. Maya Angelou said, "When you know better, you do better." I want to know better so I can do better.

I approach my desire for community the same way I approach that dance class.

I'd prefer to make a fool out of myself with the more seasoned professionals because I'm willing to stand alongside them and out myself as an amateur. I'd rather look back a year from now or ten years from now on my uncertainty as I struggled to write this book than to only have written about easy topics because they were safe. My uncertainty is proof that I was trying to grow.

We have to consider if there are areas where we stay safely inside the lines we've drawn or those drawn for us by our family of origin. And how can we know the *right* community to seek out if we've never been a part of it before? Will you treat me differently because of one of my beliefs? Will you decide that we can't be friends if we have a difference of opinion? Ask yourself this question: Is it possible that the conversations we might have together, the questions we might wrestle with, the postures we'll have to adopt in order to engage in a meaningful relationship, would help us grow into better versions of ourselves?

One of my best friends is gay, African American, and Mexican American. Three incredibly powerful narratives have shaped the woman she is, and there is so much strength, history, beauty, confidence, pain, empathy, anger, truth, and courage in her story. What if I'd never heard it? Me, the girl who once stared at a couple in Disneyland years ago as if they were on exhibit. Me, who once *often* used the phrase "That's gay" as derogatory. Me, who used to live inside a bubble where I never interacted with girls who weren't white. What if I had stayed there? What if we hadn't intentionally looked for a church that was multicultural so our children wouldn't be raised with the same homogenized worldview that we were?

What if I hadn't asked my friend to happy hour that first time? What if she hadn't been unendingly gracious with me when I said things or asked things that I now understand were hurtful? What if we didn't have the kind of relationship where she could call me out and lovingly explain why that particular phrase was offensive? What if I hadn't been willing to sit within the discomfort of working through a lifetime of unconscious bias? What would that mean for my work, my children, and what they grow up believing is true? Beyond just what I learned, what about what I received? What about the countless hours we've laughed until our sides hurt? What about the nine million memes we've tagged each other in? What about the shoulder to cry on for both me and Dave when we walked through our adoption process? What about vacations and movie nights and that one time we saw Britney Spears in concert? It would all be lost. So much love and wisdom and friendship would still be sitting on the other side of that line in the sand.

A few years ago one of Dave's friends was in town with his family, and they were coming over for dinner. It was the first time I would meet this friend and his wife and the first time our boys would meet their son. Their son is still, without question, the coolest person I know. We don't get to hang out with him often since they live in another state, but every time we do I'm blown away by how funny and wise and strong he is. That first time I didn't know much about him; I only knew that he was differently abled. I didn't know if he had a wheelchair or a walker, and I worried about how to make him feel comfortable in our home. I wondered about how I should prep the boys in advance—my fear being that they would ask inappropriate questions or say something unintentionally offensive to our new friends. Should I talk to them about his differences and explain that they didn't matter? Should I make sure they understood that friends are friends regardless of how they look or get around? Should I explain everything I could about his abilities so they wouldn't ask more?

I had so many questions and so much uncertainty as I considered explaining his condition to my boys—but then I realized something. I was about to teach my children to draw a line in the sand. I was about to point out the things that made our new friend different and therefore *other*. After all, in my own childhood, the invisible, enforced divide between "us" and "them" (intentional or not) made others seem wrong. So that day I chose to say nothing at all except that a new friend was coming over to play. When our buddy arrived on the scene, they thought his walker was the coolest thing ever. They begged him to let them try it out. They ran up and down the hallway testing out all its features. They'd never had a playdate with someone with different abilities, but that day it didn't occur to them that it was unique. I've seen this happen again and again over the years as we've met friends with Down syndrome or autism or cerebral palsy. Their circle of friends is made up of every color, religion, and ability, and they come from every kind of family. Different isn't unique to them; different is their normal. There are no lines in our sandbox.

There isn't one right way to be a woman. There isn't one right way to be a daughter, friend, boss, wife, mother, or whatever else you categorize yourself as. There are so many different versions of each and every style on this planet, and beauty lives in that dichotomy.

The kingdom of God is in that dichotomy.

At the end of every one of my hip-hop dance classes, the room breaks into smaller groups so we can watch each other perform. It's every kind of person from every walk of life and we're all sweaty and gross, but we sit down beside each other to cheer on the others. Imagine that: a large group of people who are committed to doing the hard work together, joining in to simply cheer on a community. You can see the beauty in that, right? And that's not even the best part. The best part about this time together is the difference in everyone's interpretation of the beats. We all learned the exact same moves (well, *they did*, but there's no telling what I might bust out), but every person's dance looks different from everyone else's. The girl who grew up doing ballet has movements that are more fluid and graceful. The guy who knows how to break-dance rocks a style all his own. We're all practicing the same thing . . . but we do it in different ways.

Our different styles are beautiful to behold.

What if we don't presume to know the answers? What if we're always asking questions? What if we don't settle for the world we feel comfortable with, but push ourselves to seek more? It would mean that we would find true relationship with other women at a soul-deep level instead of a skin-deep perception.

We do not need to change our entire belief system to make this a reality. We can simply adjust our posture to consider a wider, more inclusive community.

If we adjust our posture, it will change the way we speak.

If we adjust our posture, it will change the way we listen.

If we adjust our posture, we will see the person, not the category they fall into.

This is true of race, religion, political affiliation, sexual orientation, socioeconomic background, and any other category we can dream up. Doing life with people who don't look or think or vote like us is the whole point—it's our call to arms! Love thy neighbor wasn't a suggestion; it was a command, you guys. How in the world are you going to love your neighbor if you don't *know* your neighbor? I don't mean waving hello at the grocery store; I mean actually pushing ourselves outside of our comfort zone and *doing life* with different kinds of people . . . even if we wonder if they're getting it all wrong. Heck, *especially if we think they're getting it all wrong.* We need to be in a wider community not because we're attempting to sharpen their clarity on a subject but because we're hoping to soften the edges of our own hearts.

What does your story look like? Is it filled with all the same colors and lines? Do all the characters in your book look and act like each other? Imagine what would happen—imagine how beautiful the same scene might appear, what it would mean for your worldview or your *children's worldviews*—if you added different hues, different narratives, different dialogues. What would it mean to challenge your outlook every now and again? What would it mean for your relationship with your own understanding if you had to ask more questions? How would it affect other people's behavior if they saw your unbiased, open heart welcoming new friends? What could we accomplish in our communities if we took all the energy that we typically spend drawing lines and used it instead to draw our neighbors closer?

Every day you get to choose the way your world looks. Regardless of how you were raised or what you were taught to believe, you get to decide where your story goes from here. Look at the pictures in your book . . . Are they all one color?

Every year you close a new chapter in your story. Please, please, *please* don't write the same one seventy-five times and call it a life.

THINGS THAT HELPED ME . . .

1. *Changing churches.* Dave and I looked up one day and realized that we went to an affluent church in Bel Air and that 99.9 percent of our church family was white. This is not what the body of Christ looks like. The body of Christ is every color and style and background. By seeking out a church that was intentionally multiethnic, multicultural, and intergenerational, we were able to find real community.

2. *Acknowledging my position.* It's not easy to admit that you've done things or said things or believed things that were

hurtful—particularly when you weren't even aware of them; but if you don't admit to the problem, how will you ever change? Look around you: How much diversity do you see? Are you surrounded by people who are *exactly* like you? If so, begin to seek new friends and experiences.

3. **Asking humble questions.** My dear friend Brittany has been an incredible teacher for me in so many ways because she allows me to ask questions about race and white privilege and unconscious bias that could potentially be hurtful in my ignorance. She told me once, "Rachel, I'm never going to be offended if you ask the question. I only get offended if someone who isn't my race just assumes they know the answer." So I ask questions . . . and I ask them humbly.

CHAPTER 20

The lie:

I NEED A HERO

At least one of my chapters should have the same title as a classic eighties song, right? Come on, don't pretend you don't remember that scene in *Footloose* where they battle each other on the back of a combine. It's epic. It also has nothing to do with this next subject, but I love to remember Kevin Bacon's illustrious film career whenever possible.

Speaking of bacon . . .

I was a little chubby as a child.

And not that one necessarily tied in with the other (or maybe it did), but I also wasn't what anyone would call "athletic." I was the president of the drama club, a preteen who stayed in Girl Scouts long after it was cool, a card-carrying member of the FFA. That's the Future Farmers of America, for any of you who didn't grow up in God's country.

I tried on a few sports for size. One awkward year I somehow made it onto my high school tennis team . . . but my only real memory of that season is the tennis pictures we took, where I had a big hole in my sock that I didn't notice until the pictures came out. So much for enticing boys with wallet-sized pics of me in my sister's hand-me-down tartan skirt.

I was never more than mediocre at any sort of sport, and honestly, I didn't really mind. We all have our gifts, and mine are far, far removed from the athletic field.

Then, years ago when I was pregnant with our third son, Dave trained and ran a half marathon. I know what you're thinking because I was definitely thinking it too. What kind of *monster* decides to get in epic shape for the first time while his wife is the size of one of those tiny homes on HGTV?

Dave Hollis, that's who!

He looked so good and had so much energy, and I was so jealous I could spit! While running long distance wasn't something I had ever aspired to do, the fact that I *couldn't* do it because of my swollen belly irked me.

The next year when he planned to run that same race again, I jumped on board. The joke is, if you'd have asked me at any point in my life before then, I would've happily told you how much I *hated* running. But while I might not be an athlete, I am competitive. I wanted to prove to myself I could run thirteen miles without dying . . . just as he had done. I wanted to prove to our boys that daddies *and* mommies can be strong and powerful. I also sort of wanted to see if I was actually lacking in athletic prowess or if maybe that was just something I had always believed about myself.

So I started training for a half marathon—which, if you're curious, is like running in sand while wearing a backpack full of pudding.

Everything is hard. Everything feels awkward. Every single new mile makes you want to puke. But I didn't give up, and slowly—so stinking slowly—I got stronger and better, one quarter-mile at a time.

As it turns out, I'm actually a really good long-distance runner. I have short little legs, so Dave (or basically anyone) can beat me in a sprint all day long. But here's the deal: *very* few people (and I can say this confidently) can *mind-over-matter* themselves as well as I can. I've lived through fifty-two hours of labor. I've built a company from the ground up using street-smarts and the cash from my day job. I've built my life on not giving up on the goals I set for myself. So if I say I'm going to run thirteen miles, I am darn well going to run thirteen miles!

That means when mile six hits and Dave wants to quit and start walking, I fly right past him, tortoise-and-the-hare style.

The very first half marathon I ever signed up for was a Disney race. As a sidenote, *please, please, please* do yourself a favor and make it a life goal to run in a Disney race! They have 5Ks, 10Ks, and half marathons, and I don't think I've ever experienced something so uplifting and fun. It's important to note the fun element because I walked into the race that morning so afraid of how hard it was going to be that I thought I would barf. But at a Disney race, there's too much magic to barf!

The races take place inside and around the parks, so you're running by rides and princesses and floats. Other runners are dressed as Disney characters and stopping for photos along the way . . . and it's just *joyful*.

Also, having run in other half marathons many times since, I can tell you that the encouragement in these races is unmatched. There is something incredibly touching about thousands upon thousands of people coming together to run toward a common goal. There were people in wheelchairs and others who were severely overweight. There were people who were eighty-five years old and young babies being pushed in strollers. There were *pregnant women*, you guys! Freaking beautiful, in-shape, pregnant women who were running over ten miles with a full belly. I was in awe! Everywhere I turned I saw people actively challenging themselves to be something better—and it was a beauty to behold. We were one giant, sweaty mass of hope, made up of people from all walks of life who'd dreamed this dream and found themselves on the road together.

With that many people, it takes a while to make your way to the start of the line, but when my queue was called up, they started playing "A Dream Is a Wish Your Heart Makes" from Cinderella over the loudspeakers. I know it sounds cheesy in the retelling, but, y'all, I was bawling by the time it was my turn to run. I kept thinking, *This is a wish my heart made!* And for once I didn't beg off or get lazy or stop trying . . . I did it!

Running thirteen miles is really tough, and later, when I trained and ran my first full marathon, I thought I was going to die.

Straight. Up. Die.

Sometimes within the race I'd see a mile marker and take a selfie of me leaping across to show how great I was feeling. Other times it took everything I had to put one foot in front of the other. But it was during that first half marathon—mile eleven, to be exact—that I struggled the most. I kept scrolling through my iPod to find a song that would fire me up, because by that point I'd listened to or skipped over every tune I had. I landed on "I Need a Hero" by Bonnie Tyler . . . I love me some eighties music, and this one gets me going every time. It did the trick. I was feeling a little better and picking up my pace as I started to sing along with Bonnie . . .

"*I need a hero . . .*"

As any child of the eighties knows, the whole song is about her looking for a man, a hero, a "streetwise Hercules to fight the rising odds," and there I was singing along at the end of mile eleven when I had one of the biggest epiphanies of my adult life:

I don't need to find anyone. Right now, in this moment, I'm my own hero.

It was a profound realization in my life. I had pushed myself to do something I never thought I could be capable of, and it lit a fire within my own soul. Nobody forced me to put in those miles. Nobody woke me up in the morning and made me research the right shoes or which GU packets were least disgusting. Nobody else got the sunburns or the blisters or saved up to pay the entrance fee.

That was all me.

And the things *you've* achieved? The big and little stuff that peppers your life and adds flavor, the achievements that have made you who you are—those are *all you.*

I heard once that every author has a theme, and they basically just write the same message over and over in each book despite the plot or the characters. This is absolutely my truth, even if I was totally oblivious to it at the time.

Every book I've ever written is based on this core theme of my life. It's the lesson I've learned over and over again, so it inevitably weaves its way into my stories—and this book especially.

It is the gift I wish I could give every person I know.

It is the thing I wish someone had taught me as a child. Instead, I had to navigate life and figure it out on my own.

It is the greatest lesson I have to give you.

Only *you* have the power to change your life.

This is the truth. I ran an entire marathon with Philippians

4:13 written on my hand in Sharpie, and I believe that my Creator is the strength by which I achieve anything. But God, your partner, your mama, and your best friends—none of them can make you into something (good or bad) without your help.

You have the ability to change your life. You've *always* had the power, Dorothy. You just have to stop waiting for someone else to do it for you. There is no easy way out of this; there is no life hack. Just you and your God-given strength and how much you desire change.

I hope, pray, wish, cross my fingers and my toes that you will look around and find an opportunity to be your own hero. Every woman should feel that kind of pride, but if you're seeking change you shouldn't just want that for yourself, you should *need* it. You need to set a goal for yourself and then work your butt off to get there. I don't care if that goal is to pay off your credit card or lose ten pounds or run an Iron Man. You need to make a move *right now* while you're still on fire from this book about what goal you're setting for yourself. Then you need to *go do it*. You need to prove to yourself that you can do it. You need to prove to yourself that you are capable of anything you set your mind to.

You have the power.

You, exhausted mother of three who's considering heading back to work but is afraid she's been out of the loop too long. You, fifty pounds overweight and conscious that your health is in jeopardy if you don't make drastic changes. You, in your early twenties who wants love but gives away your body in order to feel connection and instead only feels emptier. You, who wants better relationships with the people you love but can't let go of your anger in order to get there. You, all of you, any of you. Stop waiting for *someone else* to fix your life! Stop assuming that someday it will magically improve on its own. Stop presuming that if you only had the right job, the right man, the right house, the right car, the right *whatever* that your life will become what you've always dreamed of. Be honest about who you are and what you need to do to make change.

Girl, get ahold of your life. Stop medicating, stop hiding out, stop being afraid, stop giving away pieces of yourself, stop saying you can't do it. Stop the negative self-talk, stop abusing your body, stop putting it off for tomorrow or Monday or next year. Stop crying about what happened and take control of what happens next. Get up, right now. *Rise up* from where you've been, scrub away the tears and the pain of yesterday, and start again . . . Girl, wash your face!

ACKNOWLEDGMENTS

First and foremost, I have to thank you, my Chic Tribe. Years ago I started blogging about what I ate for dinner, and even then, when my pictures sucked and I had no idea what I was doing—even *then* I found a community of supportive women online. When I self-published my first book, you were there. When I nervously (and awkwardly) went on TV for the first time, you were there. When I tried Instagram or danced on YouTube or told embarrassing stories in Rach Talk, you were there. And now we're here . . . with this book and this platform and this incredible community of hundreds of thousands of women all over the world—and that's because you are still here. Thank you, thank you, thank you, friends, for showing up for me and with me again and again. I believe we can change the world together . . . I believe we already have.

I am grateful as always to my mentor and champion—who also happens to be my literary agent, Kevan Lyon. Kevan, I'm not sure if you had any idea what you were getting yourself into when you took that first phone call with me, but I'm so stinking thankful you've come along for the ride.

Thank you to the incredible, hardworking team at Thomas Nelson and HarperCollins for taking on this project. Thanks, too, for the cheddar biscuits and chips and guac and wine and dessert and all the untold snacks and group dinners yet to be.

On average I spend at least six months of the year writing and/or editing a book, which means six months of mood swings, outlines, verbal processing, and caffeine-induced hysteria as I work to meet a deadline. I could not do any of this without the help of an incredible, incomparable team at Chic who keeps the train moving forward even when the conductor is in a fetal position in the corner crying over book edits. Thank you, thank you, thank you to everyone at Chic HQ who continues to help me build this dream.

Endless thanks to Johana Monroy, who has loved and cared for our family for years. People ask me how I do it all, and the honest truth is, I absolutely don't. Behind the scenes is an incredible, loving friend and sister who takes care of my kiddos when work or travel takes me away from them. Jojo, I literally don't know how we would do life without you.

Thank you to my children: Jackson, Sawyer, Ford, and Noah. I'm so grateful that God allowed me to be your mommy . . . It is the greatest honor of my life.

Thank you to my husband, Dave Hollis, who allowed much of our story to be retold—not just in this book but over the last eight years of public life—even when the retelling was difficult. I am blessed to be married to someone who believes as deeply as I do in vulnerability and the power of "me too."

Lastly a significant thank you to my parents. I am truly grateful for the pieces I carry of both of you that have made me the woman I am today. Our life might not have looked like anyone else's; it was at times joyful and painful and chaotic and magical and good and hard, but I wouldn't change it. I am who I am because of who I come from. I love you both.

ABOUT THE AUTHOR

Rachel Hollis is a bestselling author, TV personality, in-demand speaker, and founder and CEO of Chic Media, the foremost authority on premium digital content for women. Named one of *Inc. Magazine*'s "Top 30 Entrepreneurs Under 30," Rachel uses her infectious energy to empower women to take control of their lives and pursue their passions without fear. Motivational, inspirational, and always approachable, Rachel's tell-it-like-it-is attitude is a refreshing approach that allows her to authentically connect with millions of women around the world. Rachel has worked with top brands to create innovative and compelling content for Chic Media's award-winning women's lifestyle blog. Rachel is the author of the bestselling

Girls Series, including *Party Girl*, *Sweet Girl*, and *Smart Girl*, as well as a cookbook, *Upscale Downhome*. Rachel resides in Los Angeles with her husband and four children. For more information, visit TheChicSite.com.